PROVERBS

for

TRADERS

Ancient Wisdom for Today's Financial Market

VINCENT RODRIGUEZ

PROVERBS
—— *for* ——
TRADERS

Ancient Wisdom for Today's Financial Market

ENDORSEMENTS

"Vincent Rodriguez has a wonderful book in *Proverbs for Traders*. By combining the ancient wisdom of Solomon with the experience of a modern day wealth maker, Rodriguez has proven that true knowledge is timeless when appropriately applied. If you live and work in the financial arena and want to increase your wealth, knowledge, and ability to share with those in need, then buy this book for yourself and like-minded friends. *Proverbs for Traders* will make you financially healthy, compassionately wealthy, and infinitely wise."

Ellie Kay
America's Family Financial Expert ®
Best-selling financial books author, including *Living Rich for Less*
Television financial guest personality
www.elliekay.com

"Vincent Rodriguez expresses on paper what overflows out of his heart. He has an intense passion for God and loves how God's word draws people into His Kingdom. *Proverbs for Traders* challenges each of us to receive from God as He comes through in extraordinary ways in our trading and our everyday life."

Douglas Goeckel
Technical Trading Institute
www.technicaltradinginstitute.com

"I found *Proverbs for Traders* to be a clear, concise, and effective tool to cultivate a firm foundation for trading and life. It affords one the opportunity to examine one's motives, ambitions, and inner principals and to make adjustments accordingly."

J. Main
Former stock broker

"I think the chapter on freedom from demonic influences in trading will be a great help!!!"
Lori Byrne
Community Life Pastor, Bethel Church, Redding, California
www.loveaftermarriage.org

"Awesome! Well done! The chapter on freedom from demonic influences in trading is well thought out, direct, clear and very concise. I trust that Vincent's straightforward approach will be an asset to those who read it. I believe the subject is extremely pertinent to the trading industry and therefore will yield good fruit in those who read and apply it into their lives."

Debbie Adams
Counselor, Transformation Center, Bethel Church, Redding, California
Heart of Heaven Ministries, www.heartofheavenministries.com

DEDICATION AND ACKNOWLEDGMENTS

This book is dedicated to you who God has called to trade; to you who are partnering with God to see His kingdom come and His will be done here on earth as it is in heaven; to you who are compelled by the Father's love to bring blessings to those in need.

This book would not be what it is without the time I spent in God's presence with the Redding Kingdom Traders in our weekly meetings, and without Doug Goeckel's training in day trading.

I acknowledge the following people's contributions, which brought about significant revisions and additions to this book: my friend Amy, my editor Christina Files, and my sweetheart Chrystal. Come to think of it, this book may not have been written if Amy had not told me she felt God wanted me to read Proverbs.

I owe a debt of gratitude to the following people, who had no idea their teaching and prayer models would contribute to the contents of a book on finances: Lori and Barry Byrne (founders of the Love after Marriage ministry) and Mike and Debbie Adams (founders of Heart of Heaven Ministries).

I am grateful to Robert and Barbara Wales and the members of the Option Hunters in Saratoga, California, for not letting me quit trading when I was discouraged.

Thanks to Kathy Rodriguez for the author headshot.

Thanks to Brad Webster for his cover design and for his patience with me in the process.

A big thanks to Aaron McMahon, author of *How To Write & Publish Your Book*, for teaching me how to write and publish my book, and for employing his extraordinary ability to encourage new authors.

I also acknowledge the authors listed in the Bibliography for their contributions to my understanding of trading.

Finally, I acknowledge the work of two ancient authors whose work formed the basis for this book: King Solomon, who wrote Proverbs, and *"Jesus, the author and perfecter of faith"* (Hebrews 12:2).

CONTENTS

INTRODUCTION

King Solomon was the *International Man of the Year* for 40 years. He was the wisest and wealthiest person on earth from 970-931 BC. During his peaceful forty year reign his annual income, by some calculations, was 25 tons of gold—about $1.5 billion in US Dollars, totaling 60 billion over his 40 years—not including his profits from merchants and traders, and tributes he received from visiting kings and governors. His estate supported his seven hundred wives of royal birth and three hundred concubines. He owned a fleet of ships, and he was an international trader of lumber, quarried stones, horses, and other goods. The temple he built was probably the most expensive building per square foot in history; all the interior walls were overlaid with gold. His intellect was expansive. He wrote 3,000 proverbs and 1,005 songs (see 1 Kings 4:32). He taught botany and zoology (see 1 Kings 4:33). His reputation for great wisdom was known all over the world. *"All the earth was seeking the presence of Solomon, to hear his wisdom which God had put in his heart"* (1 Kings 10:24).

Solomon encountered God early in life, and God promised Solomon any one request. Solomon asked for wisdom to govern God's people. This choice so pleased God that He not only gave Solomon wisdom, but God also promised Solomon wealth and honor like no king before or after him. Many of Solomon's proverbs teach wisdom about obtaining wealth, and they also address how one's heart and finances affect each other.

SHORTLY BEFORE BEGINNING this book, I returned to an old habit of daily reading a chapter of Proverbs, and I started noticing verses that applied to trading. I wrote down what I observed, thinking only of improving my personal trading so it could become consistently profitable. After several days of reading Proverbs and taking notes about passages that applied to trading, I realized I was writing a book.

As I continued writing, I was often overwhelmed with a sense of God's presence as He helped me understand how Proverbs affect me as a trader. I never knew He was so concerned about my finances. Even if I compartmentalize my life, He does not. God is concerned with every area of my life. He wants to bless my entire life.

Because God met with me so powerfully as I wrote this book, I believe He will meet with you as you use it. As you apply yourself to gain wisdom, I expect God will not only give you wisdom for gaining material wealth, but He will also give you wisdom that will open up springs of life in your heart. As you grow in wisdom, it is my hope you will connect your heart and your trading—so you can trade with all your heart.

God transformed several areas of my heart as I began applying Proverbs to my trading. The most dramatic change was freedom from a five-year trading gambling addiction. A few years ago the addiction cost me tens of thousands in trading losses, the loss of my house, and the loss of a high-paying government job. Proverbs brought God from my spiritual life into my practical finances. His wisdom brought sanity to my trading. I didn't even recognize I had an addiction until Proverbs made me aware that something was wrong. Here is what happened.

A few months before I starting writing this book, I had gone through an intensive three month, six-day-a-week, day trading class. The instructor encouraged us to stop trading for the day after 3 trades so we wouldn't get emotionally out of control. I had personally committed to keep that rule. Then one day, I made 35 trades. There were times when I had lost more than my daily limit, but I couldn't stop trading. There were times when I was at or near breaking even, but I couldn't stop trading. There were times when I was profitable, but I couldn't stop trading. This compulsive behavior came out of hiding, like a pirate ship that blew my self-control out of the water.

At this point, I had studied Proverbs 1:23 and journaled about it (found in Week 5, The Value of Losses). Wisdom started speaking to me. I felt Wisdom's offer as real as if she were a person with flesh and bones, standing before me, holding out a written contract. Wisdom impressed on my mind, *"Turn to my reproof, Behold, I will pour out my spirit on you"* (Proverbs 1:23).

So I turned to Wisdom's reproof in written form. I used an entire page to write a detailed account of my suddenly recognizable shortcomings. Then I wrote that I now expected Wisdom to pour out her spirit of trading wisdom on me, as she had offered. Then I signed and dated the paper.

The next morning, from about 3:30 to 4:30 A.M., I had an encounter with God. I did not see Him or hear His voice, but I was overwhelmed spiritually and physically by a sense of His presence. He was doing something on a subconscious or heart level. Prayers and declarations flooded out of me from some deep place. Maybe it was some sort of reprogramming. I believe God set me free from a spirit of gambling.

After the US market opened that morning and I returned to trading, I realized God had pulled the gambling addiction out and replaced it with peace and self-control. My trading had been transformed—no, it was *me* that had been transformed. I recognized that day that I had been trading addictively by gambling on the stock market for the previous 5 years. You may think it strange that I had never identified my gambling addiction, despite losing money, my house, and my job. But if you have had an addiction, you will understand. I thought gambling addictions only happened in casinos and at horse races.

I already had the benefit of a personal relationship with the One whose wisdom is recorded in Proverbs before I began applying Proverbs to my trading. That relationship was foundational in enabling me to hear and respond to Wisdom's voice. I believe people without such a relationship with God can still get limited help from Proverbs—but why limit yourself? (If you would like to go beyond natural limitations and begin your personal relationship with God, please see Maximizing Wisdom, beginning on page 223.)

Wisdom is capitalized many places in this book. The Spirit of Wisdom is one of the manifestations of the Spirit of God and so refers to God; when used as such, it is capitalized in this book. Scriptural support for the Spirit of Wisdom as a manifestation of God follows:

- ❖ Wisdom is specifically listed as one of the manifestations of the Spirit of God. *The Spirit of the LORD will rest on Him, **The spirit of wisdom** and understanding, The spirit of counsel and strength, The spirit of knowledge and the fear of the LORD* (Isaiah 11:2).

- ❖ Wisdom speaks. All of Proverbs 8 is about Wisdom speaking. Verses 1-3 state that Wisdom speaks, then verses 4-36 record Wisdom's words. The relationship King Solomon had with the Spirit of Wisdom was such that he could hear Wisdom speak so clearly he was able to write what she spoke.

The wisdom contained in the book of Proverbs becomes relevant *as you apply it to specific areas* in your life. *Proverbs for Traders* has already done some of the application work for you by selecting and paraphrasing proverbs in a way that is both specific to traders and consistent with the proverb's essence.

Daily reading and application assignments are grouped to correspond with 5-day trading weeks, including a weekend wrap-up session. Wisdom tells us: "*Blessed is the man who listens to me, Watching **daily** at my gates, Waiting at my doorposts. For he who finds me finds life and obtains favor from the Lord*" (Proverbs 8:34-35). Would you like to find Wisdom? Would you like to obtain favor from the Lord? Working through the daily assignments in this book will help you watch and wait for Wisdom.

For maximum benefit:
- ❖ Interact with God as you go through this book; Wisdom is an aspect of God's Spirit, so you can grow in wisdom as you fellowship with Him.

- ❖ Apply yourself to the worksheets. They may be more beneficial to you than what you read in the book. The worksheets, not the text, are the heart of the book.

- ◈ Go though the course with a small group of traders, meeting weekly. It is an intense course, and you will be more likely to complete and benefit from it in a group.

- ◈ Repeat the course several times.

- ◈ Between the times you take the course, work through Part 2 and 3 of this book, or take a month to go through the entire book of Proverbs, reading and meditating on one chapter a day.

I have experienced God and received much help in my personal life during the processes necessary to write this book on Proverbs. Yet it undoubtedly contains flaws in reasoning and communication, gaps in knowledge, and incomplete understanding. It is simply what I have initially mined and found to be helpful from King Solomon's Proverbs and from God's Spirit of Wisdom. And so I offer for your consideration the understanding I possessed at the time of publication. For many it will also be *your* beginning point for fresh encounters with God and with His spirit of Wisdom, to spark your own insights and lead to your own applications and benefits beyond these pages.

May your trading bring you into a life of deeper fellowship with your Creator. May you become a blessing to more people than you ever thought possible.

Wisdom and peace,

Vincent Rodriguez

For free accompanying resources go to proverbsfortraders.com

PURPOSE OF THIS BOOK— THE HEART OF TRADING

*T*echnical trading is the basis for short term active trading, swing trading, and day trading; it primarily employs your mind to trade. *The psychology of trading* can dramatically improve success in trading when used in addition to the understanding of technical methods; it teaches you how to utilize the broader resources of your soul (your mind, your will, and your emotions). *Proverbs for Traders* is a ground-breaking work in a new field I call "the heart of trading."

The heart of trading teaches you how to trade using the additional resources of your spirit: the spirit is the deepest level of your being, where your strongest hindrances or abilities reside. For example, the psychology of trading can help you understand and avoid gambling tendencies that are driven by your thinking, your will, or your emotions, but addressing how to get free from a gambling addiction lodged in your spirit is outside the scope of that field. To be precise, *the heart of trading* actually deals with both the soul (mind, will, and emotions) and the spirit, but it is the only trading approach I am aware of that primarily addresses your spirit. The purpose of *Proverbs for Traders* is to help you establish a *spiritual* foundation for success in trading.

Faulty spiritual foundations can undermine any expertise you gain in technical trading methods and in the psychology of trading. A spiritual foundation of *wisdom and righteousness* will not only support your technical and psychological trading abilities but will provide *spiritual* trading tools and abilities as well. Just as there is some overlap between the psychology of trading and technical trading methods, there is also overlap between *the heart of trading* and the psychology of trading.

Establishing a solid spiritual foundation does not automatically guarantee success in trading. Good spiritual foundations establish tools and eliminate hindrances to success at the foundational level of your being. You must still gain expertise in technical trading methods and gain what you need from those who teach the psychology of trading.

Additionally, you should seek God to determine if trading is a part of His plans for you. Why would you want to undertake or continue any endeavor without the assurance of God's blessing on it, especially for anything as difficult as trading? *"Unless the LORD builds the house, They labor in vain who build it"* (Psalm 127:1).

Contrary to what many amateur traders expect, I know of three professional traders who compare the effort required to become a successful trader to the effort required to become a lawyer, a doctor, and an Olympic athlete. Some people try their hand at trading thinking it is a way to make money quickly, without realizing it is a profession. You will need a great passion and a solid assurance that you are meant to trade in order to carry you through the arduous process of becoming a consistently profitable trader.

Proverbs for Traders will help you gain a spiritual foundation of wisdom and righteousness, freedom from demonic influences, and spiritual trading tools.

Proverbs makes a clear connection with wisdom and prosperity. God's Spirit of Wisdom speaks to us in Proverbs and gives us inside information on the path to prosperity so people who have a personal relationship with God can prosper and not be in want. So, if wisdom brings prosperity and it is God's will for His children to prosper, **why are so many not prospering?** I offer the following reasons for your consideration.

- ❦ Lack of wisdom: many people don't adequately seek or apply wisdom.

- ❦ Lack of planning and faith to prosper: If you are not planning and expecting to prosper, you likely will not prosper.

- ❦ Individual calling: Jesus certainly had the wisdom to become wealthy, but his personal calling required devoting his entire life to its accomplishment. Some people are called and choose to devote their lives to a purpose that does not include extensive financial endeavors. (It should be noted here that although Jesus did not establish streams of business or investment income, Jesus *was not poor* as traditionally pictured. He had the financial means and backing, the financial freedom, to support *three years* of travel and ministry, for himself and his ministry team, without working, owning a business, or investing.)

- ❦ Love of money: God may be protecting you from being ruined by money, if you currently love or trust money more than Him.

- ❦ Lack of national wisdom: If a nation does not have the fear of displeasing the Lord (which leads to corruption and oppression) and lacks just laws that give citizens the opportunity to profit from their initiative and hard work (such as the right to own land and businesses and to not be overtaxed), the national environment is anti-prosperity in law and in spirit. It will not have an economy that supports individual wealth, nor will it have the favor and blessing of God to produce wealth.

So, are you obtaining and applying the Spirit and the teachings of Wisdom? Do you have plans and an expectation to prosper, and are you diligently implementing those plans? Does your purpose in life allow for the pursuit of prosperity? Do you love and trust God more than money? Do you live in a country that allows its citizens to own land, own businesses, and which has laws that do not unreasonably prevent or tax profits? Many of these things will be addressed as you work through this course.

For free accompanying resources go to proverbsfortraders.com

BEFORE BEGINNING THIS COURSE, ANSWER THE FOLLOWING QUESTIONS

What would you like to gain from this course?

_____
_____
_____
_____
_____
_____
_____
_____

Ask God what He would like you to gain from this course. Wait a moment for Him to communicate with you. Write down what He shows you.

_____
_____
_____
_____
_____
_____
_____
_____

Has God spoken to you about trading before? Ask God to confirm if He wants you to be trading. What did He communicate to you?

_____
_____
_____
_____
_____
_____
_____

PART 1

DAILY MEDITATIONS AND WORKSHEETS

WEEK 1

GOD WANTS YOU TO PROSPER

*But if anyone does not provide for his own, and especially for those of his household, he has
denied the faith and is worse than an unbeliever.*

1 Timothy 5:8

*A good man leaves an inheritance to his children's children, and the wealth of the sinner
is stored up for the righteous.*

Proverbs 13:22

He who shuts his ear to the cry of the poor will also cry himself and not be answered.

Proverbs 21:13

God's design is that heads of households would provide for their aged parents, themselves and their spouse, their children, leave an inheritance for grandchildren, and help the poor. How could you do that unless you prosper? Since God instructs you to provide for four generations of your family line and to help the poor, His will is that you would prosper.

If you don't fully believe God wants to bless you with wealth, if you don't understand the good that wealth can do in the hands of the righteous, if you secretly fear that wealth may ruin you, or if you believe that money is the root of all evil, your beliefs will not support your efforts at trading.

First Timothy 6:10 says the *love* of money, not money itself, is the root of all kinds of evil. Proverbs 10:22 says it is God's blessing that makes people rich. God gave riches to Job, Abraham, Isaac, Jacob, Joseph, David, Solomon and others; Jesus used government issued money to pay for his expenses, the expenses of his ministry team, and his taxes—so money itself *cannot* be evil.

Proverbs contain God-given wisdom and therefore convey His perspective. Where do your current beliefs on money and wealth come from? Are you teachable enough to consider God's wisdom recorded in Proverbs concerning wealth? Will you continue to leave the wealth of the world only in the hands and under the control of unrighteous, unjust, and oppressive people?

MEDITATION 1

I love those who love me; And those who diligently seek me will find me. Riches and honor are with me, Enduring wealth and righteousness. My fruit is better than gold, even pure gold, And my yield better than choicest silver. I walk in the way of righteousness, In the midst of the paths of justice, To endow those who love me with wealth, That I may fill their treasuries.

-The Spirit of Wisdom, as recorded in Proverbs 8:17-21

Trader's Paraphrase

I, Wisdom, love traders who love me; and traders who diligently seek me will find me. I bring riches, honor, generational wealth, and I transform hearts to make them right. My benefits are more desirable than pure gold and the best silver. I walk with traders who walk on the right path, and I endow traders who love me with abundant wealth.

Wisdom has greater benefits than wealth, but Wisdom also gives wealth. There is no logical or interpretive basis for accepting the Spirit of Wisdom's stated association with righteousness and honor but rejecting her association with wealth. Wisdom wants to endow you with generational wealth for a family line trained to generate and handle wealth. Generations of wealthy families who have right hearts are a powerful means for reversing injustice and for displaying God's goodness.

It is a mistake to be unwilling to believe Scripture's plain language, and to fail to appropriate the wealth associated with Wisdom, due to anti-wealth thinking derived from experiences in your life, in your culture, in history, or in the Church. You must examine your beliefs with humility and make the necessary changes to fit with God's wise perspective.

RESPONSE 1

Response: What are my thoughts? What is God saying to me?

_____
_____
_____
_____
_____
_____
_____
_____
_____
_____

Brainstorming: What are 5 possible applications?

_____
_____
_____
_____
_____
_____
_____
_____
_____
_____

Application: What one application will I put to use today or this weekend?

_____
_____
_____
_____

MEDITATION 2

It is the blessing of the Lord *that makes rich, and He adds no sorrow to it.*

Proverbs 10:22

Trader's Paraphrase

God's blessing makes traders rich without ruining their lives.

God's blessing makes people rich—what is your reaction to that truth? He made sure it was written down in Scripture so you would know it. Is today's proverb saying that God has blessed everyone who is rich? No. The second part of the proverb distinguishes between those who are rich because of the blessing of the Lord and those who are rich without the Lord's blessing. Apart from God, riches often come with heartache. We all know of rich and famous people whose lives are filled with sorrow by the circumstances and choices their riches made available to them. But riches that result from the Lord's blessing are truly a blessing; they abundantly provide for personal and family needs and give the opportunity to help others in many ways. Your heart is blessed, not twisted, by increased resources and opportunities.

There is no culturally negative feeling associated at all with the idea of a blessing. But there are mixed feelings about riches, because riches bring mixed results. Riches are a resource that can do much evil or much good. Because bad news sells, the rich you hear about most are often associated with bad things. But here in Proverbs, as well as in other places in Scripture, God informs you that His blessing makes people rich.

Why not make a list of all the negative feelings and fears you have about personally being rich. Then put today's proverb in one hand and your questions in the other and bring them both to God and see what happens.

RESPONSE 2

Response: What are my thoughts? What is God saying to me?

_____

_____

_____

_____

_____

_____

_____

_____

_____

Brainstorming: What are 5 possible applications?

_____

_____

_____

_____

_____

_____

_____

_____

Application: What one application will I put to use today or this weekend?

_____

_____

_____

_____

MEDITATION 3

The reward of humility and the fear of the Lᴏʀᴅ are riches, honor, and life.

Proverbs 22:4

Trader's Paraphrase

If you realize that trading success is achieved with the help of God and others, and if you trade with the fear of displeasing God, you will be rewarded with God-given riches, true honor, and a full life.

Why would God give you this proverb that explains that humility and the fear of the Lord bring riches, honor, and life, unless He wanted you to have humility and the fear of the Lord so you could receive riches, honor, and life? Riches, honor, and life are a reward, and humility and the fear of the Lord bring about that reward. (See page 173 for an explanation of the fear of the Lord.) If you trade with humility and the fear of the Lord, Scripture says you may expect riches, honor, and life.

If this proverb is a departure from your belief that God has a negative attitude toward wealth, maybe it is time to depart from that belief. This proverb not only promises riches and honor but life. Life, in part, is the ability to enjoy the riches and honor God gives you. Wealth obtained and used apart from humility and the fear of the Lord can bring great ruin, but wealth obtained and used in humility and the fear of displeasing God brings great blessing to you and to others.

Do you believe God would prefer you to have humility or arrogant pride? The fear of displeasing Him or the fear of displeasing people? Honor or shame? Life or death? Riches or poverty? You already believe God wants you to have humility and the fear of the Lord, so why not choose to believe now that He wants you to have riches, honor, and life?

RESPONSE 3

Response: What are my thoughts? What is God saying to me?

_____

_____

_____

_____

_____

_____

_____

_____

_____

Brainstorming: What are 5 possible applications?

_____

_____

_____

_____

_____

_____

_____

_____

_____

Application: What one application will I put to use today or this weekend?

_____

_____

_____

MEDITATION 4

Great wealth is in the house of the righteous, but trouble is in the income of the wicked.   Proverbs 15:6

Trader's Paraphrase

Great wealth is in the house of the trader whose heart is right, but traders whose hearts are wrong will have financial trouble.

What is your gut level reaction to today's proverb? Does it raise questions? How do you view this Scripture in light of the righteous people you know who are not wealthy? One reaction some might have to a Scripture that doesn't fit with their understanding of reality is to assume it means something else. What if it means exactly what it says and there is a lack of understanding about it in your thinking, in the Church, or in an entire culture? Scripture speaks of righteousness in two ways: a person who is declared and made righteous as part of his or her initiation into a new life in God and a lifestyle of habitually lived-out righteousness empowered by God. Proverbs typically addresses the behavioral, lived-out righteousness. So then, the first half of this proverb could be saying: *Those who do the right things out of a right heart get the right results.*

So what does the righteousness that brings a person wealth look like? You may be doing right in your financial endeavors by having a well-defined and compelling vision, by developing and employing strategic planning, and by working prudently and diligently—but you may be tolerating unrighteous things in your heart such as a self-focused life, a love of money, fear, or other known or unknown areas that are not right. Righteousness that brings wealth includes doing the right things out of a right heart in all areas of your interconnected life. The only way you can live righteously in all the areas of your life is by grace through faith, and by depending on the ability and motivation that come from God's Spirit living and working in you.

RESPONSE 4

Response: What are my thoughts? What is God saying to me?

_____

_____

_____

_____

_____

_____

_____

_____

_____

Brainstorming: What are 5 possible applications?

_____

_____

_____

_____

_____

_____

_____

_____

Application: What one application will I put to use today or this weekend?

_____

_____

_____

MEDITATION 5

Honor the LORD from your wealth and from the first of all your produce; so your barns will be filled with plenty and your vats will overflow with new wine.

Proverbs 3:9-10

Trader's Paraphrase

Honor the Lord regularly from your trading wealth and annually from the first profit of each market you trade; the results will be financial abundance.

This proverb is built on the premise that God wants you to prosper and that you have wealth or are actively working to obtain wealth. This proverb is also built on the concept of working some capital asset with the potential to fill barns and vats. Their capital asset was land, and a trader's capital asset is money; their barns and vats were built to hold the produce of the land, and a trader's financial accounts are the "barns and vats" that serve to hold trading profits.

Then we get some spiritual financial advice: honor God by giving away some of your income. The language suggests two things. Honoring God "from your wealth" consists of giving a tithe (a tenth) of all your regular income (See Deuteronomy 14:22). Honoring God "from the first of all your produce" relates to an offering called "first fruits" which consisted of the first harvestable portion of each annual crop (See Exodus 23:19). A trader's first fruits equivalent would be the amount of the first profitable week from each market you trade (each financial crop that produces a harvest). You honor God financially by giving to His spiritual institutions (primarily the Church you are a part of) and to the poor.

Although this proverb coincides with biblical Law, it is not primarily reinforcing Law, but teaching wisdom. Abraham and Jacob both gave a tithe prior to the Law (see Genesis 14:20; 28:22). Honor God with your finances, and He will bless them.

RESPONSE 5

Response: What are my thoughts? What is God saying to me?

_____
_____
_____
_____
_____
_____
_____
_____
_____

Brainstorming: What are 5 possible applications?

_____
_____
_____
_____
_____
_____
_____
_____

Application: What one application will I put to use today or this weekend?

_____
_____
_____

WEEKEND ONE
MEDITATION RESULTS

Improvements in My Thinking

_____
_____
_____
_____
_____
_____
_____
_____
_____
_____
_____
_____

Improvements in My Trading

_____
_____
_____
_____
_____
_____
_____
_____
_____
_____
_____
_____
_____

WEEKEND ONE
APPLICATION RESULTS

Day 1 Application Results

_____

_____

_____

_____

Day 2 Application Results

_____

_____

_____

_____

Day 3 Application Results

_____

_____

_____

_____

Day 4 Application Results

_____

_____

_____

_____

Day 5 Application Results

_____

_____

_____

_____

WEEK 2
GOD WANTS YOU TO HAVE WISDOM

Before looking at Proverbs that apply to wisdom in specific areas, let's use our second week to discover how much God desires to give you wisdom. When you are convinced God has wisdom waiting for you, it will establish a basis for pursuing and obtaining it by faith. Proverbs 1:2 states that the purpose of Proverbs is, "to know wisdom." God did not give you a *whole book* of Scripture on any other virtue or spiritual trait besides wisdom. What does that say about the importance He places on wisdom and His desire for you to have it?

Isaiah 11:2 says one of the manifestations of the Spirit of God is the Spirit of Wisdom. Proverbs 8:22-31 tells us Wisdom was beside God as a Master Craftsman when He created the universe, the earth, and people. Therefore, everything concerning your life was put together with wisdom. Wisdom knows how everything in life works, including the financial markets and the people who participate in them. The One who created you wants you to understand how your life was designed to function, so He gave you a collection of proverbs to reveal the foundation of wisdom upon which human life is built.

Contrary to popular belief, life actually does come with an instruction manual: the book of Proverbs.

MEDITATION 6

How blessed is the man who finds wisdom and the man who gains understanding. For her profit is better than the profit of silver and her gain better than fine gold. She is more precious than jewels; and nothing you desire compares with her. Long life is in her right hand; in her left hand are riches and honor. Her ways are pleasant ways and all her paths are peace. She is a tree of life to those who take hold of her, and happy are all who hold her fast.

Proverbs 3:13-18

Trader's Paraphrase

How blessed is the trader who finds wisdom and gains understanding. For her profit is better than the profit of trading precious metals. She is more precious than gemstones; nothing you desire even compares with her. Wisdom brings you long life, riches, honor, peace, and quality of life. And everyone who holds wisdom close is happy.

If God did not want to give you wisdom, why would He describe wisdom in such a way as to make you salivate over its benefits? And He would not tell you it is better than anything else you desire if He had not made it available to you. God wants you to have wisdom, so He describes it in a way that will inspire you to pursue it.

In what way is the profit of wisdom better than the profit you can get from trading gold and silver, and more to be desired than even great riches? Certainly you are not so naive as to believe that wealth itself will make you happy. Wealth without wisdom can leave you quite disillusioned and unfulfilled. Wisdom is better than anything you desire because it enables you to improve and enjoy everything in your life: trading, finances, health, career, relationships, serving others—everything.

RESPONSE 6

Response: What are my thoughts? What is God saying to me?

_____
_____
_____
_____
_____
_____
_____
_____

Brainstorming: What are 5 possible applications?

_____
_____
_____
_____
_____
_____
_____
_____

Application: What one application will I put to use today or this weekend?

_____
_____
_____
_____

MEDITATION 7

Wisdom has built her house, she has hewn out her seven pillars; she has prepared her food, she has mixed her wine; she has also set her table; she has sent out her maidens, she calls from the tops of the heights of the city: "Whoever is naive, let him turn in here!" To him who lacks understanding she says, "Come, eat of my food and drink of the wine I have mixed. Forsake your folly and live, and proceed in the way of understanding."   Proverbs 9:1-6

Trader's Paraphrase

Wisdom has sent an open invitation for a feast of perfect trading wisdom. The invitation is for all traders who realize they lack understanding and are ready to forsake their old trading ways.

Maybe you do not think of yourself as a naive trader or you have never seen your trading as foolish. But do you consistently make a weekly, monthly, or annual profit? Do you trade "by the seat of your pants"? Do you let your losers run and cut your winners short? Is hope one of your strategies? Have you traded for years without consistent success, or would you like greater success? Does over-trading cause you to lose money? Do you ever find yourself trying to trade your way out of a hole after losing your limit for the day, week, or month? (It is foolish to be trading without an appropriate daily, weekly, or monthly loss limit.) Do you continue to trade after making a reasonable profit, then end up losing? (It is also foolish to be trading without a system for protecting profits. We will look at how to establish loss limits and a system for protecting profits in Part 2.)

Wisdom has invited you to a feast of trading wisdom. There is a place set and reserved with *your name card* on it. Wisdom wants you to have all you need to succeed. The only things she asks is that you admit you need help and are ready to abandon your faulty trading ways. If you accept the terms, take your seat!

RESPONSE 7

Response: What are my thoughts? What is God saying to me?

_____
_____
_____
_____
_____
_____
_____
_____
_____

Brainstorming: What are 5 possible applications?

_____
_____
_____
_____
_____
_____
_____
_____
_____

Application: What one application will I put to use today or this weekend?

_____
_____
_____
_____

MEDITATION 8

He stores up sound wisdom for the upright.   Proverbs 2:7

Trader's Paraphrase

God stores up flawless wisdom for traders who are committed to what is right.

Did you know God has sound, reliable, flawless trading wisdom stored up for you if you are committed to what is right? He also has wealth stored up for you (see Proverbs 13:22). Are you beginning to get the idea that God is not only willing, but *yearning*, to be good to you? David knew this when he wrote, "***Surely*** *goodness and lovingkindness will follow me all the days of my life*" (Psalm 23:6). Isaiah 30:18 says, "*The* LORD ***longs*** *to be gracious to you.*"

Some people believe they have to bend the rules to prosper. They think that only those who are a bit dishonest, a bit greedy, and a bit willing to sell their soul will get ahead in the dog-eat-dog financial world they are familiar with. What a limited perspective! While it is true that some people do get wealthy in underhanded ways, their wealth will at most only benefit them in this life, if it does not ruin their lives in the process. But the wisdom that God gives helps you build wealth with righteousness and peace, and blesses your relationship with Him, blesses your life and your family, and sets you up to partner with God in blessing others. Sound wisdom doesn't just bring isolated financial success but success and satisfaction in all areas of your interconnected life.

The Creator of wealth offers you wisdom to obtain the wealth He has stored up for you. God is love. He created you to love you. He created you to live and prosper by wisdom. He inspired Proverbs to help you find wisdom. If you aren't actively expecting God to help you obtain His financial wisdom and favor, why not let today's proverb begin to change your expectations?

RESPONSE 8

Response: What are my thoughts? What is God saying to me?

_____

_____

_____

_____

_____

_____

_____

_____

Brainstorming: What are 5 possible applications?

_____

_____

_____

_____

_____

_____

_____

_____

Application: What one application will I put to use today or this weekend?

_____

_____

_____

MEDITATION 9

Wisdom cries aloud in the street, in the markets she raises her voice.   Proverbs 1:20 (ESV)

Trader's Paraphrase

Wisdom is calling out on Wall Street; in the financial markets she speaks loudly.

Since ancient times, the street has been a place where people set up markets, where people buy and sell, where trading of money and commodities occurs. When choices are made concerning business and money, the heart is often affected and its motivations revealed. God cares for you and is very concerned about your heart, so He speaks His wisdom loudly to you as you are trading. Are you hearing what Wisdom is saying? What is a practical way of hearing Wisdom's voice, as she is crying aloud?

I passed by the field of the sluggard and by the vineyard of the man lacking sense, and behold, it was completely overgrown with thistles; its surface was covered with nettles, and its stone wall was broken down. **When I saw, I reflected upon it; I looked, and received instruction.** *"A little sleep, a little slumber, a little folding of the hands to rest,"* then your poverty will come as a robber and your want like an armed man. Proverbs 24:30-34

As Solomon observed and reflected on a specific situation, Wisdom instructed him. What is happening in your mind, in your emotions, and in your spirit as you trade? What are the results of the specific trades you take? As you observe and reflect on your heart and your trading, expect God to teach you how to hear what Wisdom is saying.

Also, practice listening for Wisdom to speak plainly and directly to your mind or spirit. Just because you are not hearing does not mean Wisdom is not speaking.

RESPONSE 9

Response: What are my thoughts? What is God saying to me?

_____

_____

_____

_____

_____

_____

_____

_____

_____

Brainstorming: What are 5 possible applications?

_____

_____

_____

_____

_____

_____

_____

_____

Application: What one application will I put to use today or this weekend?

_____

_____

_____

MEDITATION 10

They would not accept my counsel, they spurned all my reproof. So they shall eat of the fruit of their own way and be satiated with their own devices. For the waywardness of the naive will kill them, and the complacency of fools will destroy them.   Proverbs 1:30-32

Trader's Paraphrase

Traders who reject wise advice, and turn away when their mistakes are pointed out, will be filled with the disastrous results of trading their own way. For the naive stray from the path of success, and the foolish do not take the action required for success.

You have already read that Wisdom cries aloud to bless you with trading counsel. God so loves you, and so much wants your trading and your life to work out, that He gives you additional motivation to seek wisdom by letting you know the tragic results of not actively seeking wisdom and acting with wisdom. Some aspects of God's will are going to happen *whether or not* people cooperate. Other aspects of His will are only going to happen if people *do* cooperate. Scripture says it is God's will that everyone is saved, but that does not happen for everyone. Just because God has stored up wisdom for you does not mean you will automatically receive it. He informs you of what He wants for you, so you can pursue it.

Today's proverb speaks of rejecting wisdom two ways: actively rejecting Wisdom by rejecting Her counsel and reproof to you or passively rejecting Wisdom by not seeking wisdom or by being too complacent to apply the wisdom you have acquired. Your options are success or failure: pride, which comes before the fall, or humility, which leads to blessing. It is not enough just to become familiar with the sayings of the wise. You must actively seek and daily choose to act with wisdom, or you are rejecting wisdom by default.

RESPONSE 10

Response: What are my thoughts? What is God saying to me?

_____
_____
_____
_____
_____
_____
_____
_____

Brainstorming: What are 5 possible applications?

_____
_____
_____
_____
_____
_____
_____

Application: What one application will I put to use today or this weekend?

_____
_____
_____
_____

WEEKEND TWO
MEDITATION RESULTS

Improvements in My Thinking

_____
_____
_____
_____
_____
_____
_____
_____
_____
_____
_____
_____
_____

Improvements in My Trading

_____
_____
_____
_____
_____
_____
_____
_____
_____
_____
_____
_____
_____

WEEKEND TWO
APPLICATION RESULTS

Day 6 Application Results

_____

_____

_____

_____

Day 7 Application Results

_____

_____

_____

_____

Day 8 Application Results

_____

_____

_____

_____

Day 9 Application Results

_____

_____

_____

_____

Day 10 Application Results

_____

_____

_____

_____

WEEK 3

VISION TO ENERGIZE YOUR TRADING

Vision will energize your trading with purpose and passion. Vision will pull you through challenges and unlock new abilities. Vision will lift you out of mediocrity and drive you to excel. Vision will propel you to obtain the blessings stored up for you and the ones you love. Vision will motivate you to become what God created you to be and do what He created you to do. Vision will help you fulfill your destiny.

This week we are going to look at five areas of vision for your trading.

MEDITATION 11

*A **worker's** appetite works for him, for his hunger urges him on.*   Proverbs 16:26

Trader's Paraphrase

A Trader's financial needs work for him, for they urge him on.

Unmet and reoccurring need urges you on. Have you ever thought that not having enough to meet your needs could be a blessing in disguise? Unmet daily needs, or losing your job, house, or business can urge you on to success. Many of us never have the determination necessary to change our financial situation without first coming to a point of desperation. Your physical hunger can work for you by urging you on when you would rather not work so hard. Unmet needs and extended desperate situations may be the very things that propel you into abundance.

God can use your financial needs to drive you into your financial destiny. He can use your past or current failures as launching pads for prosperity. Are you in need of additional income to meet your immediate or future needs? Are you in debt? Do you and your family have to go without basic necessities? Maybe you have turned to trading for similar reasons. Maybe you have lost money in trading that you could not afford to lose, creating an even more desperate situation. So why not turn that desperation into vision to change your personal financial situation permanently?

On the following page, write a vision for your *personal* finances (we will address family inheritance, giving, ministry, and other areas during the next four days this week). Today just focus on your *personal* financial vision, including you and your immediate family only. Next, brainstorm and listen to God. Then write out possible steps to turn that vision into reality. Finally, commit your initial plan to God so He can begin working it out with you.

RESPONSE 11

My Personal Financial Vision (for me and my immediate family)

_____
_____
_____
_____
_____
_____
_____
_____
_____
_____

Brainstorming: How could this vision be fulfilled?

_____
_____
_____
_____
_____
_____
_____
_____
_____
_____

Application: Preliminary step-by-step Plan

_____
_____
_____
_____

MEDITATION 12

A good man leaves an inheritance to his children's children, and the wealth of the sinner is stored up for the righteous.   Proverbs 13:22

Traders' Paraphrase

A good trader leaves an inheritance to his family line, and the wealth of those who err from what is right is stored up for traders who do what is right.

Do you consider yourself a good person? Today's proverb says good people leave an inheritance substantial enough to help their grandchildren begin their own efforts in becoming financially established. It is a good thing for people and families whose hearts are right to have generational wealth. Good people use wealth for good. Do your plans currently include leaving a financial inheritance to a family line trained to generate and handle wealth?

This proverb is not intended to make you feel guilty. It is written to let you know how things are meant to be. Today's proverb tells us good people are meant to know how to produce and handle wealth. If that doesn't fit with your beliefs, why not change your beliefs? You will tend to rise or fall to the level of your beliefs. (Hopefully you don't pull your beliefs down when you are down.) Proverbs are given to correct and instruct your thinking. If you and your family line or circle of friends believe it is right for good people to make just about enough money to meet their needs that is probably what you have experienced in your life. If you believe that good people prosper, that is probably what you have experienced.

On the following page, write a vision for your family inheritance. What if you left enough for each grandchild to get an education or establish a business that will enable them to build wealth? Next, brainstorm and listen to God. Then write out possible steps to turn that vision into reality. Finally, commit your initial plan to God so He can begin working it out with you.

RESPONSE 12

My Family Financial Inheritance Vision

_____

_____

_____

_____

_____

_____

_____

_____

_____

Brainstorming: How could this vision be fulfilled?

_____

_____

_____

_____

_____

_____

_____

_____

_____

Application: Preliminary step-by-step Plan

_____

_____

_____

_____

MEDITATION 13

By the blessing of the upright a city is exalted.   Proverbs 11:11

Trader's Paraphrase

The blessing of traders committed to what is right can lift an entire city.

The upright in each societal area of influence (business, government, family, religion, media, education, and entertainment) are positioned to lift their social and geographical arenas out of things like poverty, violence, injustice, and corruption, by displacing the dominion of Satan with the dominion and Kingdom of God by replacing a curse with a blessing. When the upright bring blessing to multiple areas of influence, whole cultures and geographical regions are transformed. It has happened in the past and it is happening now in various places and countries around the world. God put this verse in Scripture to let you know that a group of God's upright traders have a part in giving a blessing that will break the influence of darkness and transform whatever city or communities they are a part of. If you thought a call from God to trade was just about providing financially for you and your family, widen your vision!

The love of money is the root of all kinds of evil. If those in places of cultural and governmental influence are held by the of love money, evil will be released over the area they influence or govern. But when those who love righteousness and people, instead of money, begin to use financial resources and influence to bless a culture, city, or nation, it will be set free and lifted up.

On the following page, write a vision to lift a culture, city, or nation. Next, brainstorm and listen to God. Then, write out possible steps to turn that vision into reality. Finally, commit your initial plan to God so He can begin working it out with you.

RESPONSE 13

My Vision to Lift up a Culture, City, or Nation

_____

_____

_____

_____

_____

_____

_____

_____

Brainstorming: How could this vision be fulfilled?

_____

_____

_____

_____

_____

_____

_____

_____

Application: Preliminary step-by-step Plan

_____

_____

_____

_____

MEDITATION 14

Do you see a man skilled in his work? He will stand before kings; he will not stand before obscure men.   Proverbs 22:29

Trader's Paraphrase

Do you see a trader skilled in his work? He will influence people of authority and influence; his place will not be among unknown people.

If you are a skilled trader, you will be influential. Most people are happy to receive an annual return of just a few percent on their money. If your monthly return is what most people get annually, people will hear about you and seek you out.

The level of skill that brings people to stand before kings (literal kings, as well as those who are in places of authority and influence) is an uncommon skill level. Top-level professional athletes and concert pianists, world-class inventors in medicine and technology, and those with uncommon financial and business expertise are examples of the kind of abilities that capture the attention of influential people.

Uncommonly excellent skill takes an uncommonly excellent endeavor. It takes uncommon vision to fuel an uncommon drive. Successful trading takes uncommon excellence in practice, diligence, and focus, and an uncommon willingness to eliminating things that steal time, energy, and resources. It takes an uncommon commitment to success. Why not decide to do what it takes to become an excellent trader who is skilled in your work?

On the following page, write a vision to influence the influential. Next, brainstorm and listen to God. Then write out possible steps to turn that vision into reality. Finally, commit your initial plan to God so He can begin working it out with you.

RESPONSE 14

My Vision to Influence People of Influence and Authority

_____
_____
_____
_____
_____
_____
_____
_____
_____

Brainstorming: How could this vision be fulfilled?

_____
_____
_____
_____
_____
_____
_____
_____
_____

Application: Preliminary step-by-step Plan

_____
_____
_____
_____

MEDITATION 15

Deliver those who are being taken away to death, and those who are staggering to slaughter, Oh hold them back. If you say, "See, we did not know this," does He not consider it who weighs the hearts? And does He not know it who keeps your soul? And will He not render to man according to his work? Proverbs 24:11-12

Trader's Paraphrase

Use your trading to free those held in death's grip. If you pretend you don't see them, doesn't God know your heart? And won't He give you the just results of your choices?

We who have been blessed with access to more financial resources than we need have additional means to save those who are in the grip of physical and spiritual death. Many people would turn to God, avoiding eternal death, if someone would share the good news that Jesus gave His life to give them a new one. Giving to organizations that deliver people from eternal death will give an eternal return on your investment and bring joy to your heart now as you spend your life on a purpose and a Kingdom greater than your own.

There is another application of today's proverb: delivering people from an earthly, living death caused by things such as human trafficking for sexual or labor slavery, abortion (death of the undesirable unborn), genocide (death of members of races considered undesirable by those with the military or political power to kill), and starvation.

On the following page, write a vision to deliver those being taken away to death. Which individuals or group being held captive by death most stirs your compassion to set them free? Next, brainstorm and listen to God. Then write out possible steps to turn that vision into reality. Finally, commit your initial plan to God so He can begin working it out with you.

RESPONSE 15

My Vision to Rescue People from Death

_____

_____

_____

_____

_____

_____

_____

_____

Brainstorming: How could this vision be fulfilled?

_____

_____

_____

_____

_____

_____

_____

_____

Application: Preliminary step-by-step Plan

_____

_____

_____

_____

WEEKEND THREE MEDITATION RESULTS

Improvements in My Thinking

_____
_____
_____
_____
_____
_____
_____
_____
_____
_____
_____
_____

Improvements in My Trading

_____
_____
_____
_____
_____
_____
_____
_____
_____
_____
_____
_____
_____

WEEKEND THREE
APPLICATION RESULTS

Day 11 Application Results

_____

_____

_____

_____

Day 12 Application Results

_____

_____

_____

_____

Day 13 Application Results

_____

_____

_____

_____

Day 14 Application Results

_____

_____

_____

_____

Day 15 Application Results

_____

_____

_____

_____

WEEK 4
GUARDING YOUR HEART

Don't forget about your heart while trading. First Timothy 6:9-10 illustrates the potential riches have to ruin people:

But those who want to get rich fall into temptation and a snare and many foolish and harmful desires which plunge men into ruin and destruction. **For the love of money is a root of all sorts of evil**, *and some by longing for it have wandered away from the faith and pierced themselves with many griefs.*

The primary focus of these verses is not riches but your heart. If becoming rich materially is more important than becoming rich spiritually, you open your life to temptations, traps, foolish and harmful desires, and being *plunged* into ruin and destruction. Loving money leaves your heart unguarded. Is your temporary, earthly life more valuable to you than your eternal, spiritual life? You must intentionally invest your life now in the eternal Kingdom of God, or you will spend your life on this temporary world by default.

The warning against the love of money does not cancel out the proverbs concerning God's willingness to bless righteous people with wealth. Second Timothy 3:16 says that all Scripture is inspired by God and useful for training in righteousness. Second Chronicles 16:9 says, *"For the eyes of the* LORD *move to and fro throughout the earth that He may strongly support those* **whose heart is completely His."** Maybe you will be one of those He will use to bless many, because you have faithfully stewarded wealth with a guarded heart.

MEDITATION 16

Watch over your heart with all diligence, for from it flow the springs of life.

Proverbs 4:23

Trader's Paraphrase

Watch over your heart with all diligence in your trading, so the springs of life can remain open and flow freely.

There is something even more important than being diligent in your trading: being diligent in guarding your heart while trading. Your whole life flows from your heart. Your heart consists of your emotions, will, mind, and spirit, and directly affects your success in life, your quality of life, and your physical health. God made your heart so springs of life would flow freely out of it as you love Him. But the springs of an unguarded heart can be blocked up.

The intensity of trading, with its potential for producing great wealth, makes it a potent tool for revealing the affections and motivations of your heart. It reveals whether you love wealth or God. It indicates if you trust yourself or God. This diagnostic tool is a great benefit, and it may prove even more valuable to your life than trading.

Trading presents almost constant choices of trading in fellowship with God or in momentary isolation from Him. You must choose to trade trusting in God, or you default to trusting in yourself or focusing on money. The motto "IN GOD WE TRUST" is appropriately placed on American currency and coin to remind us to be on guard against the temptation to trust in money. Guard your heart with all diligence while trading, so the springs of your physical, emotional, and spiritual life will flow freely.

RESPONSE 16

Response: What are my thoughts? What is God saying to me?

_____

_____

_____

_____

_____

_____

_____

_____

_____

Brainstorming: What are 5 possible applications?

_____

_____

_____

_____

_____

_____

_____

_____

_____

Application: What one application will I put to use today or this weekend?

_____

_____

_____

_____

MEDITATION 17

He who trusts in his riches will fall, but the righteous will flourish like the green leaf.   Proverbs 11:28

Trader's Paraphrase

The trader who trusts in his riches will wither, but the trader whose heart is right will flourish.

As your trading gets more profitable, you need to guard against depending less on God. You may be tempted to subtly shift your trust from God to your success in trading. God gave His people a warning about this trap of success when they were about to enter the Promised Land:

Beware that you do not forget the LORD your God by not keeping His commandments and His ordinances and His statutes which I am commanding you today; otherwise, when you have eaten and are satisfied, and have built good houses and lived in them, and when your herds and your flocks multiply, and your silver and gold multiply, and all that you have multiplies, then your heart will become proud and you will forget the LORD your God who brought you out from the land of Egypt, out of the house of slavery.   Deuteronomy 8:11-14

Notice that the Israelites were to guard their hearts by remembering God and keeping His instructions when they gained abundance. Guarding your heart includes protecting it from slowly drifting into trusting in wealth. Keeping Wisdom's proverbs in your heart and on your mind keeps you trusting in God. The practice of daily seeking Wisdom and embracing the fear of displeasing God, the practices that built your spiritual foundation for success, will also keep your heart guarded and in a safe place. To offset the voices of this world that call daily to pull you backwards, listen daily to the voices of God that call you forward.

RESPONSE 17

Response: What are my thoughts? What is God saying to me?

_____

_____

_____

_____

_____

_____

_____

_____

_____

Brainstorming: What are 5 possible applications?

_____

_____

_____

_____

_____

_____

_____

_____

Application: What one application will I put to use today or this weekend?

_____

_____

_____

_____

MEDITATION 18

Give me your heart, my son, and let your eyes delight in my ways.

Proverbs 23:26

Trader's Paraphrase

As you trade, give your heart to your Father God and allow your eyes to enjoy His perspective.

Who do you give your heart to while you trade? What do your eyes delight in while you trade? Is your trading compulsive and disconnected from God, or is it peaceful and done in fellowship with God? Are you growing in trading with confidence, discipline, and interaction with God? Guarding your heart in trading begins with first giving your heart to God and then enjoying trading in friendship with Him. God created your eternal heart as well as your earthly capacity to gain wealth. Money doesn't care about your heart. God does.

Just as you can be in a marital relationship without a heart fully given to your spouse, you can be in relationship with God without fully giving your heart to Him. Is trading part of your fellowship with God, or does it come between you and Him? God asks you to give Him your heart for the same reason Jesus tells you to remain in His love (see John 15:9)—so He can bless you with everything and in every way His heart wants to. He wants you to have success in trading and a heart guarded against things that would harm you.

If your heart is not currently behaving as if it is fully given to God, why not give it fully to Him now? If your eyes focus on foolish trading setups, why not decide to see with His wisdom? Do you really think anything in your life will turn out better if you hold back part of your heart from God? Since loving God with all your heart is His greatest commandment for you (see Mark 12:28-30), you can be sure He will receive your heart and help you guard it as you trade.

RESPONSE 18

Response: What are my thoughts? What is God saying to me?

_____

_____

_____

_____

_____

_____

_____

_____

_____

Brainstorming: What are 5 possible applications?

_____

_____

_____

_____

_____

_____

_____

_____

_____

Application: What one application will I put to use today or this weekend?

_____

_____

_____

_____

MEDITATION 19

Trust in the LORD with all your heart and do not lean on your own understanding.
Proverbs 3:5

Trader's Paraphrase

Trust in the Lord with all your heart in every aspect of trading, realizing that your own understanding is limited.

God gave you a mind to think and a heart to discern so you could understand; so why would He tell you not to lean on that understanding? Why would he give you the capacity to develop an understanding necessary to function in the various areas of life, then admonish you not to depend on that understanding?

As humans, we are thinking and discerning beings, yet we commonly have different, even deficient, understanding. One person may have a better grasp, a more complete perspective, a superior understanding in a particular area. We often seek the advice of such experts, and when we find a good one, we will depend on their understanding rather than ours.

It is the same with God. If you find God has a different perspective on an issue than you do, why would you not trust His understanding, rather than continuing to lean on your limited point of view? His perspective is not limited by time or personal experience, as ours is. When you suspect a difference in your understanding and God's, will you choose to benefit by humbling yourself and trusting in Him? Or will you allow arrogance or rebellion to rob you of the good God wants you to have?

When you come across a proverb that conflicts with your established perspective, which will you trust? When God speaks to your heart regarding your thoughts or motivations, will you be prudent enough to consider what He is pointing out and be diligent enough to do what it takes to establish a new track to run on?

RESPONSE 19

Response: What are my thoughts? What is God saying to me?

_____

_____

_____

_____

_____

_____

_____

_____

_____

Brainstorming: What are 5 possible applications?

_____

_____

_____

_____

_____

_____

_____

_____

Application: What one application will I put to use today or this weekend?

_____

_____

_____

_____

MEDITATION 20

The crucible is for silver and the furnace for gold, and each is tested by the praise accorded him.   Proverbs 27:21

Trader's Paraphrase

Silver is refined in a crucible and gold in a furnace, and traders are refined by the praise people give them.

As people notice that you are a successful trader, you will need to guard your heart and your conversations, giving appropriate credit to God, others, and yourself. When trading brings you attention and accolades, your heart will be tested. That is a good thing. Testing shows you what has been established and gives you an opportunity to reinforce it.

People's praise will help you identify who you give credit to and who you are looking to for approval. How do you respond to comments of admiration? How do you react when people ask you for advice? Your reaction will tell you a great deal, if you pay attention to it. God can use trading for more than just financial provision for our families and for funding our visions and contributions in life; He can use trading to reveal our hearts to us. As today's proverb says, praise, especially reoccurring praise, acts on our heart just as fire acts on gold and silver; it remove our impurities and increases our beauty and our value.

Humility will act as a guard to your heart; keeping you from arrogance on one hand and from rejecting affirmation on the other. (See the section introduction to "Trading with Humility" for a description of true humility.) The next time someone compliments you on your trading success, notice your response and what goes on in your thoughts. If you prepare yourself now with an understanding of what humility really is, you will have another tool to help guard your heart from destructive pride. And you will know how to respond gracefully and appropriately when you are tested by the fire of praise.

RESPONSE 20

Response: What are my thoughts? What is God saying to me?

_____

_____

_____

_____

_____

_____

_____

_____

_____

Brainstorming: What are 5 possible applications?

_____

_____

_____

_____

_____

_____

_____

_____

_____

Application: What one application will I put to use today or this weekend?

_____

_____

_____

_____

WEEKEND FOUR
MEDITATION RESULTS

Improvements in My Thinking

_____
_____
_____
_____
_____
_____
_____
_____
_____
_____
_____
_____

Improvements in My Trading

_____
_____
_____
_____
_____
_____
_____
_____
_____
_____
_____
_____
_____
_____

WEEKEND FOUR
APPLICATION RESULTS

Day 16 Application Results

Day 17 Application Results

Day 18 Application Results

Day 19 Application Results

Day 20 Application Results

YOUR PROGRESS
THIS MONTH

Significant improvements in my thinking the past four weeks

_____

_____

_____

_____

_____

_____

_____

_____

_____

_____

_____

_____

Significant improvements in my trading the past four weeks

_____

_____

_____

_____

_____

_____

_____

_____

_____

_____

_____

WEEK 5
THE VALUE OF LOSSES

We all understand the benefit of profit. But have you ever considered the value of financial trading losses? Losses can bring you trading wisdom that profit cannot. Losses can free you from arrogance and make you teachable. Losses can help transform you in areas that success cannot. Losses can teach you to avoid loss. If you learn to gain from your losses, they will pay you back many times over.

MEDITATION 21

Turn to my reproof, behold, I will pour out my spirit on you.

-The Spirit of Wisdom, as recorded in Proverbs 1:23

Trader's Paraphrase

If you respond when I point out your trading mistakes, I will pour out my spirit of trading wisdom on you.

Would you like to have the spirit of trading wisdom poured out on you? What are Wisdom's trading reproofs, or reprimands, and how can you recognize and respond to them? A long string of losing trades; losing more per trade or per day than good risk management rules support; the loss of a significant or pre-determined percent of your trading capital—these are observable reproofs. You can also learn to recognize reproofs felt in your heart, such as identifying any unwillingness to make or keep trading rules, realizing when your trading is emotionally driven rather than system driven, or taking note of a lack of peace on an entry or exit. Of course God's Spirit of Wisdom can also speak directly to you.

Before we can respond to Wisdom's reproofs, we have to recognize them. Keep logs, journals, and/or chart pictures. Keep track of your account growth or loss. If you are not paying attention, you may not recognize when you are being reproved. Don't let pride or desperation cause you to continue draining your account. Preserve your trading capital. Stay in cash. Learn. Pray. Get counsel from others. Create or reaffirm good risk management and trading rules. Study charts. Paper trade.

Why should you continue trading and lose even more, especially if you are in financial need? Just because you need to make money trading doesn't mean you will. In the process of repenting and turning to Wisdom's reproof, you can expect Wisdom to deliver on the promise of pouring out her spirit of trading wisdom.

RESPONSE 21

Response: What are my thoughts? What is God saying to me?

_____
_____
_____
_____
_____
_____
_____
_____
_____

Brainstorming: What are 5 possible applications?

_____
_____
_____
_____
_____
_____
_____
_____
_____

Application: What one application will I put to use today or this weekend?

_____
_____
_____
_____

MEDITATION 22

Stripes that wound scour away evil, and strokes reach the innermost parts.

Proverbs 20:30

Trader's Paraphrase

Painful trading losses remove bad trading practices, and big hits to a trading account affect core trading beliefs.

There is great benefit in painful trading losses. They give you an opportunity to see and get rid of things that could further devastate your trading. Pain gives perspective. Losses can get through to you when preventative instruction does not. Once our minds have formed a belief about something, even if the belief is faulty and not well thought out, we seem to hold onto that belief unless it is substantially disproven.

Losses can be very helpful in running right over faulty but established, trading beliefs regarding a system, a market, an indicator, money and risk management rules, or the belief that you can profitably trade familiar setups without knowing the probabilities because you have seen them work many times before—that is gambling. Without losses that are consistent enough or large enough to cause you real pain, you may never discover or dislodge faulty trading beliefs and practices.

There is an aspect of learning to trade that is different from the learning you get from books or seminars, a type of learning gained only by experience and emotional impact. You can learn some things about trading by seeing, hearing, or reading instructional material. Other things must be trained into you through experience. Thank God for painful trading wounds and stinging trading strokes—the losses that scour away destructive trading beliefs and practices.

RESPONSE 22

Response: What are my thoughts? What is God saying to me?

_____

_____

_____

_____

_____

_____

_____

_____

Brainstorming: What are 5 possible applications?

_____

_____

_____

_____

_____

_____

_____

_____

_____

Application: What one application will I put to use today or this weekend?

_____

_____

_____

MEDITATION 23

When the scoffer is punished, the naive becomes wise.   Proverbs 21:11

Trader's Paraphrase

When a trader pays the price for rejecting good advice, he changes from naive to wise.

I think most of us generally tend to be wise and to benefit from sound trading instruction, while another part of us tends to scoff at wise instruction and discount it because of pride, jealousy, or the naivety that comes from inexperience. You certainly believe you are wise enough to succeed at trading or you would not be attempting to trade. And you must also feel you are somewhat naive, somewhat in need of trading wisdom, or you would not be reading this book. I point this out because your first reaction to today's proverb was probably to dismiss it as not applicable to you, since you are not a scoffer or naive.

You will be somewhat naive in any area of trading in which you are not yet an expert. Just because you are proficient in one market or type of trading, or in using certain systems or indicators, does not mean you are also proficient in areas of trading which you have not yet mastered. There are two aspects to being naive: one is simply being inexperienced and the other is too easily believing whatever side of a story you are first exposed to (such as thinking that trading was easy money because a person at a free seminar demonstrated how effective their proven method was. Yeah, that one got me too.)

Trading losses punish the scoffer in us, and they help change us from naive to wise. Pay close attention to your trading losses. Listen and look for wisdom. Then alter your beliefs and practices, so you will be sure to get your money's worth!

RESPONSE 23

Response: What are my thoughts? What is God saying to me?

_____

_____

_____

_____

_____

_____

_____

_____

Brainstorming: What are 5 possible applications?

_____

_____

_____

_____

_____

_____

_____

_____

Application: What one application will I put to use today or this weekend?

_____

_____

_____

_____

MEDITATION 24

*My son, do not reject the discipline of the L*ORD *or loathe His reproof, for whom the L*ORD *loves He reproves, even as a father corrects the son in whom he delights.*

Proverbs 3:11-12

Trader's Paraphrase

Do not reject God's trading correction or hate Him pointing out your trading mistakes; for God tells those He loves when they are wrong, like a father corrects a child he delights in.

The benefits of trading losses can go far beyond bringing discipline to your faulty or underdeveloped trading methods, and they can even do more than bring attention to faulty psychology that accompanies poor trading. Trading losses can bring corrective discipline and benefit to your heart. Books on trading usually focus on the technical, psychological, and money management aspects of trading, but what about your heart? What about how your heart affects trading and how trading affects your heart? How does the rest of your life affect your trading and how does your trading affect the rest of your life? God can use trading losses to bless you with correction regarding issues of your heart and your life. He can use trading to address things such as motivations and values, fear vs. faith, anxiety vs. peace, pride vs. humility, and issues of self-image and self-worth.

Just as you would gladly expose your trading to the scrutiny of an affirming mentor to benefit from his or her trading wisdom, expose what trading stirs up in your heart to your heavenly Father so you can benefit from His wisdom for your trading and for your whole life. Do this as you take time to work through this book and in the moment when an issue is fresh. When God reproves you, He is saying, "I love you." When He corrects you, He is saying, "You are my child in whom I delight."

RESPONSE 24

Response: What are my thoughts? What is God saying to me?

_____
_____
_____
_____
_____
_____
_____
_____
_____

Brainstorming: What are 5 possible applications?

_____
_____
_____
_____
_____
_____
_____
_____
_____

Application: What one application will I put to use today or this weekend?

_____
_____
_____
_____

MEDITATION 25

*A **man who hardens his neck after much reproof will suddenly be broken beyond remedy.***
                                                          Proverbs 29:1

Trader's Paraphrase

A trader who refuses to change after repeatedly having his mistakes pointed out will come to sudden financial ruin.

Previous proverbs showed us the benefits of paying attention to trading losses. Today's proverb warns of the ruin that comes from repeated refusal to learn from the reproof of losses. One aspect to learning to trade is finding out the beneficial results of doing or not doing something a certain way. The opposite is just as critical: finding out the *negative* consequences of doing or not doing something a certain way.

Do you keep losing without knowing exactly why? Do you allow yourself to remain in denial and to keep trading and losing month after month? Wisdom is speaking to you and offering you the benefit of her rebuke. Listen to Wisdom. Stop trading until you see. It is prudent to remain in cash and retain your trading capital until you have successful systems that are working in current-market conditions, that you have adequately back tested and paper traded, and for which you have figured the probabilities and percentages. It is foolish to keep losing.

You are not failing as a trader if you stop trading real money to study and paper trade until you gain the necessary wisdom and experience to succeed; you are moving forward. As long as you stay engaged with the processes of trying, failing, learning from failure, and readjusting, you are becoming a wise trader. You can expect Wisdom's help as you temporarily stop trading.

RESPONSE 25

Response: What are my thoughts? What is God saying to me?

_____
_____
_____
_____
_____
_____
_____
_____
_____

Brainstorming: What are 5 possible applications?

_____
_____
_____
_____
_____
_____
_____
_____
_____

Application: What one application will I put to use today or this weekend?

_____
_____
_____
_____

WEEKEND FIVE
MEDITATION RESULTS

Improvements in My Thinking

_____
_____
_____
_____
_____
_____
_____
_____
_____
_____
_____
_____
_____

Improvements in My Trading

_____
_____
_____
_____
_____
_____
_____
_____
_____
_____
_____
_____
_____

WEEKEND FIVE
APPLICATION RESULTS

Day 21 Application Results

_____

_____

_____

_____

Day 22 Application Results

_____

_____

_____

_____

Day 23 Application Results

_____

_____

_____

_____

Day 24 Application Results

_____

_____

_____

_____

Day 25 Application Results

_____

_____

_____

_____

WEEK 6
TRADING WITH DISCIPLINE

Successful traders are disciplined traders. But how did they get their discipline? The ability to act with discipline comes out of a history of receiving and learning from corrective discipline. Discipline to act comes from a firsthand process of being trained and refined through *experience*, rather than from book learning.

Rules feel limiting to those who have not received discipline by personal experience in trading. But rules don't *limit* you—they *focus* you. If you try to run through a wall, you will just bounce off. But if you apply that same energy to the wall with the head of a sledgehammer, you will see the power of focus. Discipline focuses you for success that you would otherwise never achieve.

MEDITATION 26

Let your eyes look straight ahead, fix your gaze directly before you. Make level paths for your feet and take only ways that are firm. Do not swerve to the right or the left; keep your foot from evil.   Proverbs 4:25-27 (NIV)

Trader's Paraphrase

As you trade, look only for proven setups. Develop solid trading systems and take only trades based on those systems. Do not alter your rules as you trade. Do not take other trades.

Have you considered trading with disciplined eyes? There is a time for looking at everything you can see on the charts. But how do you direct your eyes and mind *while you are trading*? While you are trading are your eyes searching only for and focusing only on your proven trading systems? Or do you let just any market move catch your eyes and pull you into a trade? Do you trade the market, or does the market trade you?

The fact that it was necessary to write a proverb urging us not to deviate from firm, level paths points out the common tendency to do just that. But we can choose to take only those paths that are firm and level.

There will always be market moves outside your style of trading. There will always be setups, entries, and exits that look good to you, and may often work out as you anticipated, but these are not trades that you have mastered and made your own. Taking a trade based on a pattern or setup that you have seen work before is very different from taking a trade based on your setups, entries, and exits that you have tested, and for which you have worked out the probabilities and percentages. Only your tested trades are "ways that are firm." You find out if a trading path is firm by testing it, by extensively back testing and paper trading it, and determining if the odds are actually in your favor. Discipline your eyes while trading to look only for your trades—let *everything else* go by.

RESPONSE 26

Response: What are my thoughts? What is God saying to me?

_____
_____
_____
_____
_____
_____
_____
_____

Brainstorming: What are 5 possible applications?

_____
_____
_____
_____
_____
_____
_____
_____

Application: What one application will I put to use today or this weekend?

_____
_____
_____

MEDITATION 27

Bind them [Wisdom's teachings] *on your fingers; write them on the tablet of your heart.*   Proverbs 7:3

Trader's Paraphrase

Use whatever external and internal means are necessary to remember Wisdom's lessons, so your trading is unavoidably accompanied by what Wisdom has taught you.

What would it take for you to consistently trade with the teaching, rules, and understanding that Wisdom has given you? How do you bind them to your fingers, so you see them every time you place a trade? By what means do you write them on the tablet of your heart so they are a part of your every trading motivation and thought?

Besides literally writing out your most important trading rules, rolling them up, and tying them to your fingers, what could you do to keep your rules and wisdom at your fingertips while you trade? Perhaps writing them out and looking at them as you enter and exit trades? What about keeping pictures next to your computer of charts that show examples of what each of your trades look like, with the accompanying trade rules written on it? What else comes to mind?

What time, place, and methods do you have for internalizing what Wisdom has taught you? If you don't have a plan, a routine, a way to imprint your acquired trading wisdom on your heart so it speaks louder to you than the ever changing price fluctuations, trend lines, and indicators—guess which will prevail? Wisdom not used will not benefit you.

Make your hands act with wisdom. Make your heart think with wisdom. Be creative or be boring, but do whatever it takes to make Wisdom's invaluable lessons an inseparable part of your trading.

RESPONSE 27

Response: What are my thoughts? What is God saying to me?

_____

_____

_____

_____

_____

_____

_____

_____

_____

Brainstorming: What are 5 possible applications?

_____

_____

_____

_____

_____

_____

_____

_____

Application: What one application will I put to use today or this weekend?

_____

_____

_____

MEDITATION 28

Whoever loves discipline loves knowledge, but he who hates reproof is stupid.   Proverbs 12:1

Trader's Paraphrase

Whoever loves corrective trading discipline loves trading knowledge, but he who hates having his trading mistakes pointed out is stupid.

Do you love having your trading mistakes pointed out? Do you keep your losing trades to yourself because you don't want people to know? To love corrective trading discipline and reproof is to love trading knowledge. Of course, you want to be selective with the people you expose your trading to. But how foolish it is to avoid seeking out the advice of expert traders. Your fellow peer traders can also offer valuable observations, if you love trading knowledge enough to give them the opportunity. They can see your trades with a different perspective than you and may help you see things you are missing.

Traders are not the only source to get reproof and corrective discipline. Wisdom herself often raises her voice as you trade in the financial markets, regularly offering you practical rebuke in the form of your trades losing more money than they are making or speaking directly to your spirit about issues of the heart or even giving you practical, technical trading tips. (I know of a trader who has dreams in which God shows technical trading methods that lead to profitable trading systems.)

If you love trading knowledge, learn to recognize the reproof regularly offered to you by expert and peer traders and by Wisdom speaking through the markets and to your heart. Learn to love the risk of exposing your trades to those who might point out your errors; you will have to decrease pride and increase humility. Or, as the proverb says, if you prefer to be stupid, just keep hating reproof.

RESPONSE 28

Response: What are my thoughts? What is God saying to me?

_____

_____

_____

_____

_____

_____

_____

_____

_____

Brainstorming: What are 5 possible applications?

_____

_____

_____

_____

_____

_____

_____

_____

_____

Application: What one application will I put to use today or this weekend?

_____

_____

_____

_____

MEDITATION 29

Poverty and shame will come to him who neglects discipline, but he who regards reproof will be honored.   Proverbs 13:18

Trader's Paraphrase

Poverty and shame will come to the trader who neglects correction, but the trader who responds when his mistakes are pointed out will be honored.

How do you know when you are neglecting discipline in trading? If your trading account balance declined last month, and you are still trading the same way, you are probably neglecting trading discipline (unless your particular trading system is designed to include negative months while making annual profits). If you enter or exit a trade outside of your experience-based rules, you are neglecting discipline.

Receiving and acting with discipline can be hard work emotionally and spiritually. You can voluntarily humble yourself to recognize and embrace discipline's correction or you can neglect discipline and be humbled against your will. The trading discipline you have received through experience is precious and belongs to you; it cost you time and money.

To receive discipline, you must first recognize it. Part of recognizing corrective discipline is keeping records of each trade in logs, in journals, or in pictures of your trades on charts, and then analyzing those records. They must be recorded in great detail, so they can be scrutinized until they yield lessons you can turn into rules and habits for trading with discipline.

Do you have to do any adjusting in the time and methods you are dedicating to receiving trading discipline and regarding trading reproof? What about using your trading time to trade less and analyze more? To regard discipline and rebuke requires *a lot* of effort. To default to poverty and shame takes less.

RESPONSE 29

Response: What are my thoughts? What is God saying to me?

_____
_____
_____
_____
_____
_____
_____
_____
_____

Brainstorming: What are 5 possible applications?

_____
_____
_____
_____
_____
_____
_____
_____
_____

Application: What one application will I put to use today or this weekend?

_____
_____
_____
_____

MEDITATION 30

Cease listening, my son, to discipline, and you will stray from the words of knowledge.

Proverbs 19:27

Trader's Paraphrase

If you stop listening to trading correction, you will stray from the trading knowledge you once possessed.

Listening to corrective trading discipline is an ongoing part of successful trading. If you don't keep paying attention to the trading discipline that Wisdom is *currently* giving you, you will stray from the trading knowledge you once had. What if a system that worked very well last year or last month is now losing money? Will you keep using it as it is, or receive correction and then find out what needs adjusting?

Who or what can Wisdom speak through? Don't overlook market action, other traders, trading books, trading results, and God's Spirit communicating to your spirit. When do you hear trading discipline? Maybe you hear when you lose money or peace, when trading or when analyzing trades, when meditating on Proverbs, or when talking with God and expecting Him to communicate with you.

Discipline is not just a current response to lessons learned in the past; it is also a current commitment to ongoing development. Furthermore, true discipline is not a stoic adherence to external rules, including rules developed by you, but an ongoing and inward choice made freely by you (kind of like grace), without a sense of external coercion (kind of like law). True discipline comes from being convinced of the benefits of acting according to lessons learned by experience. Listening to discipline is a continual way of trading, not something you just do on the way to becoming a successful trader. Current corrective trading discipline feeds your streams of trading knowledge, like snow and rain feed streams of water.

RESPONSE 30

Response: What are my thoughts? What is God saying to me?

_____

_____

_____

_____

_____

_____

_____

_____

_____

Brainstorming: What are 5 possible applications?

_____

_____

_____

_____

_____

_____

_____

_____

Application: What one application will I put to use today or this weekend?

_____

_____

_____

WEEKEND SIX
MEDITATION RESULTS

Improvements in My Thinking

_____
_____
_____
_____
_____
_____
_____
_____
_____
_____
_____
_____

Improvements in My Trading

_____
_____
_____
_____
_____
_____
_____
_____
_____
_____
_____
_____

WEEKEND SIX
APPLICATION RESULTS

Day 26 Application Results

_____

_____

_____

_____

Day 27 Application Results

_____

_____

_____

_____

Day 28 Application Results

_____

_____

_____

_____

Day 29 Application Results

_____

_____

_____

_____

Day 30 Application Results

_____

_____

_____

_____

WEEK 7
TRADING WITH DILIGENCE

Diligence is a combination of hard work and perseverance. It is following through to do whatever it takes to succeed. It is never giving up. It is faithfulness. Diligence keeps going in the face of unforeseen difficulty and discouragement. Diligence brings you across the finish line.

MEDITATION 31

The plans of the diligent lead surely to abundance, but everyone who is hasty comes only to poverty.   Proverbs 21:5 (ESV)

Trader's Paraphrase

Those who consistently trade according to detailed trading plans will have abundance, but those who trade in haste will only have poverty.

Do you have solid plans for trading? Do those plans include fully developed trading systems (see page 197), money management rules (see page 191), and details such as which markets and what hours you will trade? (See Additional Decisions on page 200.) If you are losing money month after month, consider the possibility that you need to diligently make better plans and diligently carry them out.

You may be putting in many hours trading, but if you are entering and exiting trades without knowing if the odds are in your favor, your work will only lead to poverty. You may have a small or a massive trading account, but if you do not consistently follow prudent money management rules, your work will only lead to poverty.

What does trading in haste look like? Entering a trade on every market move and every change of direction is definitely trading in haste. But so is trading based on price action, support and resistance, patterns, or indicators *unless you have fully developed systems* for doing so. Most traders trade hastily. The proof is that most traders come to poverty. If your account balance continues to decline, you have been trading in haste. Has your account balance continued to decline?

Entering and exiting trades without knowing if the odds are in your favor is haste — no matter how many years you have been trading — and is a sure path to poverty. Diligently trading with fully developed plans is a sure path to abundance.

RESPONSE 31

Response: What are my thoughts? What is God saying to me?

_____

_____

_____

_____

_____

_____

_____

_____

Brainstorming: What are 5 possible applications?

_____

_____

_____

_____

_____

_____

_____

_____

Application: What one application will I put to use today or this weekend?

_____

_____

_____

_____

MEDITATION 32

The way of the lazy is as a hedge of thorns, but the path of the upright is a highway.
                                                            Proverbs 15:19

Trader's Paraphrase

Laziness blocks progress in trading, but commitment to what is right creates a highway to successful trading.

Paradoxically, it is often easier to put out more effort. Which would you consider easier to travel on: a path covered completely with thorn hedges or a wide-open highway? Laziness allows a hedge of thorns to grow, blocking your path to forward progress. Commitment to what is right creates a highway. What would that look like applied to your trading? Are there areas of your trading where additional diligence and effort would clear out the thorn bushes of frustration and open a highway of abundance? What specific additional efforts might create an unobstructed highway for your trading?

The contrast in this proverb between the lazy and the upright implies that the upright are diligent. Wisdom does not associate with laziness, except to offer corrective discipline or rebuke. Picture it this way: the upright can walk or run because they are UP-right, whereas the lazy cannot walk because they are essentially lying down on the job. Trying to get by in trading with the least amount of hard work possible is associated with laziness, mediocrity, and poverty.

Diligence in trading employs mental and emotional energy and takes a lot of time. What springs to mind as you ask yourself what areas of your trading would improve with more energy and time spent on them? Laziness is hard on you. Diligence makes a highway for your trading.

RESPONSE 32

Response: What are my thoughts? What is God saying to me?

_____
_____
_____
_____
_____
_____
_____
_____
_____

Brainstorming: What are 5 possible applications?

_____
_____
_____
_____
_____
_____
_____
_____
_____

Application: What one application will I put to use today or this weekend?

_____
_____
_____
_____

MEDITATION 33

A lazy man does not roast his prey, but the precious possession of a man is diligence.   Proverbs 12:27

Trader's Paraphrase

A lazy trader does not analyze his trades, but diligence is a precious possession for a trader.

Can you imagine a hunter so lazy that he has a successful hunt but who does not spend the additional effort to prepare and cook what he killed? Can you picture someone just walking away and letting his hunting efforts go to waste? Similarly, can you imagine a business person so complacent that he or she conducts business each day but never keeps records or analyzes the business? Can you picture someone spending their life savings setting up a business, then not doing everything they can to succeed? Just as a diligent hunter prepares and eats his prey, and a diligent business person records and analyzes his business activities, so you as a diligent trader will benefit from keeping records and analyzing your trades. Analyzing trades after you take them will improve your trading and keep you sharp. The record of your personal trades is a valuable thing, if you are diligent enough to extract its lessons.

Today's proverb says diligence is one of your precious possessions. Have you ever thought of diligence as a possession? What is so precious about it? Diligence is the difference between good intentions and finishing well. Without diligence, your good plans will wither on the vine. Diligence is a key component in implementing your plans and obtaining your goals, and as such, it is precious.

Do you currently possess adequate diligence? If not, how will you go about developing and growing your diligence? What brainstorm ideas will you list on the following page? God made a point to recommend diligence to you, so He will certainly give you help to obtain it.

RESPONSE 33

Response: What are my thoughts? What is God saying to me?

_____

_____

_____

_____

_____

_____

_____

_____

_____

_____

Brainstorming: What are 5 possible applications?

_____

_____

_____

_____

_____

_____

_____

_____

_____

_____

Application: What one application will I put to use today or this weekend?

_____

_____

_____

_____

MEDITATION 34

If you faint in the day of adversity, your strength is small.

Proverbs 24:10 (ESV)

Trader's Paraphrase

If you give up trading when unexpected difficulties occur, your determination is weak.

Adversity comes to test your strength. Adversity tries to make you lose perspective. It attempts to distract you from your well-thought-out plans. Adversity would have you forget the progress you have already made. It tempts you to give up.

Diligence is part hard work and part perseverance. Perseverance during adversity reveals the strength of your original resolve, and adversity is an opportunity to increase the strength of your resolve. It is one thing to work hard when trading is relatively new or when your passion and enjoyment are in full swing. But when things don't work out as planned, when they take more work than you envisioned, when unexpected setbacks occur, when you are disappointed in your own performance, when you have lost a huge percent or your trading account, *then* you are facing your day of adversity.

You may have thought the moment you decided to become a trader was your moment of decision, and in a way it was. But when you feel like quitting, when you are second-guessing the wisdom of attempting to be a trader, you have come to the real point of decision—the point of reaffirming your original decision.

Perseverance during adversity *affirms* your strength. Perseverance during adversity also *increases* your strength. Continuing to be diligent in the face of adversity turns it into a benefit. Diligence during adversity is part of your training for greatness.

RESPONSE 34

Response: What are my thoughts? What is God saying to me?

_____
_____
_____
_____
_____
_____
_____
_____
_____

Brainstorming: What are 5 possible applications?

_____
_____
_____
_____
_____
_____
_____
_____
_____

Application: What one application will I put to use today or this weekend?

_____
_____
_____
_____

MEDITATION 35

Poor is he who works with a negligent hand, but the hand of the diligent makes rich.

Proverbs 10:4

Trader's Paraphrase

Negligence makes a trader poor; diligence makes a trader rich.

Like many proverbs, this one is fairly straightforward. What areas of your trading are you diligent in? What areas are you neglecting? You may be trading ten hours a day, but if you not spending your time and mental energy on the right things, you are being negligent. Diligence produces prosperity; negligence brings and maintains poverty.

He also who is slack in his work is brother to him who destroys.

Proverbs 18:9

Trader's Paraphrase

He who is slack in his trading gets the same result as if he were intentionally trying to destroy his trading account.

At first glance, relating slackness to destruction seems a bit harsh. Today's first proverb said diligence produces prosperity, and negligence brings, or maintains, poverty. Slackness and negligence are both opposites of diligence, and cause unintentional destruction.

How kind of God to encourage you by describing the benefits of diligence, and then to warn you by describing the consequences of not being diligent. So, the ball is in your court. Diligence is established one choice at a time. He would not tell you about the benefits of diligence unless He wanted to give them to you.

RESPONSE 35

Response: What are my thoughts? What is God saying to me?

_____
_____
_____
_____
_____
_____
_____
_____
_____

Brainstorming: What are 5 possible applications?

_____
_____
_____
_____
_____
_____
_____
_____
_____

Application: What one application will I put to use today or this weekend?

_____
_____
_____
_____

WEEKEND SEVEN MEDITATION RESULTS

Improvements in My Thinking

_____

_____

_____

_____

_____

_____

_____

_____

_____

_____

Improvements in My Trading

_____

_____

_____

_____

_____

_____

_____

_____

_____

_____

_____

WEEKEND SEVEN
APPLICATION RESULTS

Day 31 Application Results

Day 32 Application Results

Day 33 Application Results

Day 34 Application Results

Day 35 Application Results

WEEK 8
TRADING WITH PRUDENCE

Prudence is a form of wisdom focused on giving adequate thought to actions before taking them. Prudence not only takes into account the immediate consequences, but also the big picture, the indirect consequences, and the long-term results..

This week, we will look at how your trading affects your wider circle and how that wider circle affects your trading.

MEDITATION 36

Know well the condition of your flocks, and pay attention to your herds; for riches are not forever, nor does a crown endure to all generations. When the grass disappears, the new growth is seen, and the herbs of the mountains are gathered in, the lambs will be for your clothing, and the goats will bring the price of a field, and there will be goats' milk enough for your food, for the food of your household, and sustenance for your maidens.　　　　　　　Proverbs 27:23-27

Trader's Paraphrase

Always know the condition of your trading business, for prosperous trading does not maintain itself, nor does a condition of wealth pass to the next generation automatically. Pay close attention to your trading business and you will ensure continued provision for your household during the market's changing seasons.

How well do you know the condition of your trading business? Which practices are healthy? What needs tending right away? What measurements do you use to assess the condition of your trading and money management systems? Are you letting things go undone that would improve your business because you are settling for mediocre results?

It is prudent to put controls in place, such as: preset limits at which you will discontinue using a trading system until you fix it, preset limits on daily or weekly losses, and a preset limit for a percent loss of your account at which you will halt trading altogether for some serious adjustments. You may also find benefit in limiting the number of trades or amount of profit you will take to prevent emotionally out-of-control overtrading. If you do not set controls and limits when you have a good perspective, you may tend to continue bad practices without realizing the damage until your trading account is at a critical state. Know well the condition of your trading business, so it can provide for you and your household, now and in the future.

RESPONSE 36

Response: What are my thoughts? What is God saying to me?

_____
_____
_____
_____
_____
_____
_____
_____

Brainstorming: What are 5 possible applications?

_____
_____
_____
_____
_____
_____
_____
_____

Application: What one application will I put to use today or this weekend?

_____
_____
_____
_____

MEDITATION 37

An inheritance gained hurriedly at the beginning will not be blessed in the end.

Proverbs 20:21

Trader's Paraphrase

Betting your financial future based on early trading successes will not end well.

Many people who won millions in lotteries are now deeply in debt. The ability to consistently build a trading account is far more valuable than inheriting millions, winning millions in a lottery, or having occasional big trading wins. My first trading successes, combined with unhealthy areas of my heart, developed into a trading gambling addiction that caused me to resign from an ultra-secure government job that paid a salary in the top ten percent income bracket in the USA; I resigned so I could pursue trading full time. When it was all said and done, I ended up losing a nice town house worth two times the median house price in the USA, tens of thousands in trading, and had no income from a job. The urge to gamble is based on a belief or a feeling that you can quickly gain a large sum of money without having to prudently and consistently build it up.

Do you have a trading gambling addiction? How would you know if you did have one? Some clues may be the inability to stop trading when you continue losing or when trading is harming other areas or people in your life. You could be addicted even if you are making money. In fact, if you are addicted and profiting, it will be even harder to stop trading if you start losing.

Find another trader or a friend with whom you can be completely accountable, so you leave no place for an addiction to hide. Initiate trading limits for number of trades, profit, and loss during a time period appropriate to your style of trading (per day, week, or month). Diligence in uprooting all addictive trading practices may be a major turning point in your trading.

RESPONSE 37

Response: What are my thoughts? What is God saying to me?

_____

_____

_____

_____

_____

_____

_____

_____

_____

Brainstorming: What are 5 possible applications?

_____

_____

_____

_____

_____

_____

_____

_____

Application: What one application will I put to use today or this weekend?

_____

_____

_____

_____

MEDITATION 38

He who loves pleasure will become a poor man; he who loves wine and oil will not become rich.   Proverbs 21:17

Trader's Paraphrase

The trader who loves pleasure will become poor; the trader who loves escape and indulgences will not become rich.

Just as it is not money, but the *love* of money, that ruins many, so the *love* of pleasure keeps many people poor. The love of money and the love of pleasure compel you to act without prudence. Is the love of pleasure, escape, or indulgences causing you to squander your present or potential trading capital? For now, what pleasure could you do without? Do you need help to get free from compulsive spending or any other addictive behaviors which steal time, energy, potential trading capital, or focus? Contrast this proverb with the next one.

There is precious treasure and oil in the dwelling of the wise, but a foolish man swallows it up   Proverbs 21:20

Trader's Paraphrase

The wise trader's house is filled with expensive furnishings and many luxuries, but a foolish trader spends his trading capital.

There will come a time when your trading success will allow you to enjoy many of the pleasures you had to do without when you were building your account. The waiting may even teach you to distinguish between addictions and healthy pleasures. If you wait, prudence will repay you many times over.

RESPONSE 38

Response: What are my thoughts? What is God saying to me?

_____

_____

_____

_____

_____

_____

_____

_____

_____

Brainstorming: What are 5 possible applications?

_____

_____

_____

_____

_____

_____

_____

_____

_____

Application: What one application will I put to use today or this weekend?

_____

_____

_____

_____

MEDITATION 39

Prepare your work outside and make it ready for yourself in the field; afterwards, then, build your house. Proverbs 24:27

Trader's Paraphrase

Don't depend on trading to make a living before it consistently provides enough money to support your family.

Some traders who prematurely abandoned or stopped seeking other sources of income to make a living by trading have learned the hard way that first things are first for a reason. The route that promises to bring immediate relief from a difficult situation may not be the one you will end up liking. Trading is exciting, challenging, absorbing, and can give the adrenalin rush of a full-blown gambling addiction. Don't let the potential for large profit and the excitement of trading overwhelm the wisdom of adequate preparation and good timing.

Your "house" includes not only the physical building you live in, but also the needs and desires of your family, your entire household needs. Before you start withdrawing profits, your trading should be consistently producing monthly gains that will allow you to take those withdrawals while still growing your account. Let your account continue to grow to meet your desired present and future lifestyle and giving goals, including retirement, inheritance funds, inflation, and rising costs.

If your trading account is not yet producing profit to support monthly withdrawals, what can you do to let it keep growing? Can you keep your job? Can you get a job? Could you increase or create another stream of income? What could you do without for now? The quicker you build your trading account, the quicker you can enjoy the lifestyle and giving goals you have in mind.

RESPONSE 39

Response: What are my thoughts? What is God saying to me?

_____
_____
_____
_____
_____
_____
_____
_____
_____

Brainstorming: What are 5 possible applications?

_____
_____
_____
_____
_____
_____
_____
_____

Application: What one application will I put to use today or this weekend?

_____
_____
_____

MEDITATION 40

Have you found honey? Eat only what you need, that you not have it in excess and vomit it.

Proverbs 25:16

Trader's Paraphrase

Have you found sweet success in trading? Limit your profits to appropriate amounts, because success in excess will make you sick.

Overtrading due to the sweetness of success can make your trading sick. There is such a thing as success in excess; too much too often. Overtrading is out-of-control, emotional trading. There are two directions out-of-control trading can take you: out-of-control profits and out-of-control losses. Out-of-control profits lead to out-of-control losses. You don't want out-of-control profits; you want consistent profits.

Trading in multiple financial markets will allow you to trade twenty-four hours a day. Day trading those markets will allow you to trade *intensely* for those twenty-four hours. Just as a good hunter does not shoot at every thing that moves, but waits for the right animal and the right positional setup, a good trader waits for the exact trade setup he is looking for and stops when he has reached his preset limit.

Limits on profit and the number of trades you will take guard against the destructiveness of greed. Limits on losses preserve your trading capital. Consider setting maximum limits on things such as points, ticks, or pips gained or lost; money gained or lost; number of trades; number of contracts per trade; and trading hours. Day traders need daily limits, and swing traders need limits appropriate to the duration of their trades. Trading beyond currently appropriate limits will not benefit you. Trading is only a part of your life; don't let it consume you. Trading does not give life; it is meant to enhance it. Enjoy your trading with all your heart. Enjoy the rest of your life with all your heart.

RESPONSE 40

Response: What are my thoughts? What is God saying to me?

_____

_____

_____

_____

_____

_____

_____

_____

_____

Brainstorming: What are 5 possible applications?

_____

_____

_____

_____

_____

_____

_____

_____

_____

Application: What one application will I put to use today or this weekend?

_____

_____

_____

_____

WEEKEND EIGHT MEDITATION RESULTS

Improvements in My Thinking

_____
_____
_____
_____
_____
_____
_____
_____
_____
_____
_____

Improvements in My Trading

_____
_____
_____
_____
_____
_____
_____
_____
_____
_____
_____
_____
_____

WEEKEND EIGHT APPLICATION RESULTS

Day 36 Application Results

_____

_____

_____

_____

Day 37 Application Results

_____

_____

_____

_____

Day 38 Application Results

_____

_____

_____

_____

Day 39 Application Results

_____

_____

_____

_____

Day 40 Application Results

_____

_____

_____

_____

YOUR PROGRESS THIS MONTH

Significant improvements in my thinking the past four weeks

_____
_____
_____
_____
_____
_____
_____
_____
_____
_____
_____

Significant improvements in my trading the past four weeks

_____
_____
_____
_____
_____
_____
_____
_____
_____
_____
_____
_____
_____

WEEK 9
TRADING WITH PEACE

Does trading with peace seem like an oxymoron? Even things that are intense can be done with a tranquil heart. If you have been born of the Spirit of God through Jesus Christ, yet are trading in the flesh and not in your new spirit, then you are trading by the earthly resources of your old, disconnected, natural self, instead of by the heavenly resources of your new, eternal, spiritual self. When you trade in the flesh, fear and anxiety may often accompany your trading and rob you of the very peace you need to trade well. But the new spirit God has put within you is not a spirit given to old fears. It is a spirit equipped with ability and discipline. Second Timothy 1:7 says, *"God gave us a spirit not of fear but of power and love and self-control"* (ESV).

Psalm 23 tells us God gives provision in peace. *"He makes me lie down in green pastures"* (Psalm 23:2). Since green pastures are food to sheep, and since sheep cannot sleep when they feel a predator is after them, the psalmist is saying God gives you rest and peace surrounded by abundance. This week we look at proverbs that will help you trade from a place of peace.

MEDITATION 41

A tranquil heart is life to the body, but passion is rottenness to the bones.

Proverbs 14:30

Trader's Paraphrase

Trading with peace brings physical health, but trading with passionate emotion destroys physical health.

The way you trade affects your physical health. Trading with peace, with a tranquil heart, gives health to your physical body. Trading with passionate emotions, such as anxiety, frustration, or anger is destructive to your physical health. Your spirit, your mind, your will, and your emotions affect your physical health either positively or negatively. God has invited you to enter and remain in His rest (see Hebrews 4:8-11). As your spirit learns to remain in His rest and trade with peace, it will benefit your physical health, as well as your trading.

In addition to trading with supernatural peace, what would help you trade in natural peace? How about risking less? What about back testing more? Would analyzing your trades in detail begin to eliminate poor entries and exits, thereby building confidence and reducing anxiety? What if you postponed your trading until you fully develop your own system or fully test someone else's trading system? Perhaps paper trading successfully before putting your money at risk would increase your peace? Maybe you could increase peace by trading with a very small amount of money until you can trade larger amounts with confidence?

God is not only good at being your spiritual Shepherd, but He is also competent at guiding you while trading. People who manipulate the financial markets do not intimidate God in the least or make it difficult for Him to prosper you in your trading. Trusting in His love for you and His interest in your trading will bring peace to your heart while trading and in other areas of life as well.

RESPONSE 41

Response: What are my thoughts? What is God saying to me?

_____

_____

_____

_____

_____

_____

_____

_____

_____

Brainstorming: What are 5 possible applications?

_____

_____

_____

_____

_____

_____

_____

_____

Application: What one application will I put to use today or this weekend?

_____

_____

_____

_____

MEDITATION 42

Do not weary yourself to gain wealth, cease from your consideration of it.

Proverbs 23:4

Trader's Paraphrase

Do not wear yourself out to become a wealthy trader; do not even consider overworking yourself.

What's going on here? After all these proverbs about wealth, this one instructs us to stop thinking about gaining wealth? The cohesive collection of the book of Proverbs would not contain one lone verse that negated the rest. This verse is making an important distinction concerning the way we think and work to obtain wealth. Here are two other translations.

Do not overwork to be rich; because of your own understanding, cease! (NKJV)

Do not wear yourself out to get rich; have the wisdom to show restraint. (NIV)

So, the concept here is not to make yourself mentally, emotionally, or physically weary in your efforts to prosper. This verse is not addressing your plans to gain wealth, but rather your peace in pursuing those plans; not the goal but the way you pursue those goals. If you are weary, take a break—for an hour, for the day, or for the week.

Psalm 127:2 (ESV) says, *"It is in vain that you rise up early and go late to rest, eating the bread of anxious toil; for he gives to his beloved sleep."* God knows your limitations, including your need for rest and sleep, and tailors your life accordingly. If you step outside of your fellowship with God to pursue prosperity, you will not be operating in faith or peace. Work diligently, end your day, and then go to sleep knowing that your Father is in control.

RESPONSE 42

Response: What are my thoughts? What is God saying to me?

_____
_____
_____
_____
_____
_____
_____
_____
_____

Brainstorming: What are 5 possible applications?

_____
_____
_____
_____
_____
_____
_____
_____
_____

Application: What one application will I put to use today or this weekend?

_____
_____
_____
_____

MEDITATION 43

Better is a little with the fear of the Lord *than great treasure and turmoil with it.*

Proverbs 15:16

Trader's Paraphrase

Better is a little trading success with the fear of displeasing the Lord than great trading wealth with anxiety.

If you have been reading all the proverbs to this point, you know that the book of Proverbs considers great wealth to be a good thing, a by-product of wisdom. So this verse is not speaking against having abundance. It is clarifying that the fear of the Lord is more desirable than great profits without the benefits of the fear of the Lord; the fear of the Lord with just enough to barely meet your needs is actually a more desirable situation than just having great wealth.

Without the fear of the Lord, your heart will lack an anchor and be vulnerable to waves of turmoil. You were never made to have wealth apart from the fear and the blessing of the Lord. The full benefit is to have both the fear of the Lord and abundant provision; that is what this proverb conveys when read in the context of the collection of Proverbs.

If you are experiencing turmoil in your trading, or your trading is overwhelming your life and displacing important things or people in your life, it is an indication that you may have slipped out of the fear of the Lord. Don't let the wind and the waves distract your focus from Jesus, so that you are sinking beneath the water you were once walking on when focused on Him.

Peace is one of God's characteristics. God is never in turmoil. Nothing has power over Him or surprises Him. If you trade in the fear of the Lord, you will trade in His peace.

RESPONSE 43

Response: What are my thoughts? What is God saying to me?

_____

_____

_____

_____

_____

_____

_____

_____

_____

Brainstorming: What are 5 possible applications?

_____

_____

_____

_____

_____

_____

_____

_____

Application: What one application will I put to use today or this weekend?

_____

_____

_____

_____

MEDITATION 44

He who is slow to anger has great understanding, but he who is quick-tempered exalts folly.   Proverbs 14:29

Trader's Paraphrase

The patient trader has great understanding, but the quick-tempered trader displays his foolishness.

Does your trading easily make you angry at yourself or at the market? If so, it indicates a lack of understanding and the presence of foolishness. Anger is like a hunting dog pointing at something hidden in the bushes. You may have years of experience trading, and you may have gained a good deal of trading knowledge, but if you are regularly losing your temper in trading, it indicates there is an area you can identify and improve to trade even more successfully.

In what way does being slow to anger come from great trading understanding, and in what way does a quick temper honor trading foolishness? Understanding the characteristics of the specific market you are trading, and understanding the probabilities of the trading systems you use, leaves little reason for surprise or anger—you will not be surprised, because you know what to expect. Taking only trades you have mastered will keep you from getting angry when you take a loss or see a profitable move go by that did not fit your trading systems.

Trading with a lack of understanding is foolish. Losing your temper over taking or missing an entry or exit indicates that you may have been trading foolishly. Or maybe the trade entry was good, but you were foolish in risking an unwise percent of your account. Eliminating any foolish trading habits that are identified by anger will increase your peace in trading.

Rather than being hard on yourself for getting angry while trading, why not use that energy to turn anger into a blessing by using it to identify and eliminate foolish trading habits?

RESPONSE 44

Response: What are my thoughts? What is God saying to me?

_____

_____

_____

_____

_____

_____

_____

_____

_____

Brainstorming: What are 5 possible applications?

_____

_____

_____

_____

_____

_____

_____

_____

_____

Application: What one application will I put to use today or this weekend?

_____

_____

_____

_____

MEDITATION 45

Do not fret because of evildoers or be envious of the wicked; for there will be no future for the evil man; the lamp of the wicked will be put out.

Proverbs 24:19-20

Trader's Paraphrase

Do not be upset because of unethical traders or be envious of traders whose hearts are wrong; for there will be no future for the unethical trader, and the success of traders whose hearts are wrong will come to an end.

Seeing others obtain wealth through wickedness really bothers some traders and can pull you out of peace. You might even occasionally wonder what it would be like to be in their shoes. Many stories about the unethical rich present a skewed perspective and focus only on part of their life. Those who manipulate markets, unduly skew order fills, front run orders, and prosper from other unethical practices have only a limited form of success that will end in darkness and cut off the trader's future. If you could see their whole life, now and in the future, you would not envy them. If they could see how your life will turn out, they would envy you.

Proverbs 10:22 says, *"It is the blessing of the LORD that makes rich, and He adds no sorrow to it."* You don't need to envy traders who are prospering by unethical and immoral means, because they have no protection against the sorrow that accompanies riches without the blessing of the Lord. To have riches without God's blessing is not a blessing. If you are one who has gained riches without God's blessing, why not repent (change your mind) and trust Him with your trading now? One reason He gave us Scripture is to offer us the opportunity to change the way we think and live. Traders who build their accounts steadily with a right heart will be blessed in trading, in life, and in eternity.

RESPONSE 45

Response: What are my thoughts? What is God saying to me?

_____
_____
_____
_____
_____
_____
_____
_____
_____

Brainstorming: What are 5 possible applications?

_____
_____
_____
_____
_____
_____
_____
_____
_____

Application: What one application will I put to use today or this weekend?

_____
_____
_____
_____

WEEKEND NINE
MEDITATION RESULTS

Improvements in My Thinking

_____
_____
_____
_____
_____
_____
_____
_____
_____
_____

Improvements in My Trading

_____
_____
_____
_____
_____
_____
_____
_____
_____
_____
_____

WEEKEND NINE
APPLICATION RESULTS

Day 41 Application Results

_____

_____

_____

_____

Day 42 Application Results

_____

_____

_____

_____

Day 43 Application Results

_____

_____

_____

_____

Day 44 Application Results

_____

_____

_____

_____

Day 45 Application Results

_____

_____

_____

_____

WEEK 10
TRADING WITH HUMILITY

What has humility got to do with trading? Humility helps you remain teachable and it helps you keep your head on straight when you are trading well. True humility will guard you from the extremes of false humility and of arrogance: it will keep you from rejecting affirmation and from taking all the credit. What may seem like boasting to some may actually be true humility. Humble or arrogant statements about your trading may actually sound very similar.

So what is humility? Humility is the opposite of arrogance. Humility is a proper assessment of one's self and one's accomplishments, based on a heart that recognizes and assigns credit where credit is due—credit to God, credit to others, and credit to self. Arrogance is self-assessment based on pride and naiveté, and it recognizes and assigns credit mainly to self.

First Corinthians 4:7 says, *"For who makes you differ from another? And what do you have that you did not receive? Now if you did indeed receive it, why do you boast as if you had not received it?"* (NKJV)

You did not bring yourself into existence, and you had nothing to do with the abilities you were born with. Even your ability to develop what you have been given is something you received. Humility has less to do with acknowledging your success and more to do with who you credit for your success. God, others, and you all contribute to your trading success.

MEDITATION 46

The fear of the LORD is the instruction for wisdom, and before honor comes humility.
                                                                    Proverbs 15:33

Trader's Paraphrase

The fear of displeasing God is the basis for gaining wisdom in trading, and realizing that success is achieved with the help of God and others leads to honor in trading.

In what way does the fear of the Lord instruct you in wisdom? How does being afraid of displeasing God in your trading position you to learn wisdom for trading? The fear of the Lord keeps you connected to God. It makes and keeps your heart teachable before God and open to His wisdom. The fear of the Lord is humility toward God; it is acknowledging He is more powerful and knowledgeable than you. Trading in humility toward God will guard your heart from pride and keep you open to His wisdom in the moment. Humility and the fear of the Lord are opposites of pride.

Why does humility lead to honor? For one thing, humility enables you to show your trading to others and to learn from their suggestions. Unlike pride, humility does not feel it is a loss of self-worth to acknowledge the wisdom of others or the need for their help. Humility is healthy. Humility has the ability to honor others. When we honor others, we create an open door to receive from them.

The fear of the Lord positions you for honor by enabling you to receive His trading wisdom for success. And humility toward people positions you for honor by letting you benefit from their experiences and perspectives. You gain much by replacing any arrogant pride with humility toward God and others.

RESPONSE 46

Response: What are my thoughts? What is God saying to me?

_____

_____

_____

_____

_____

_____

_____

_____

Brainstorming: What are 5 possible applications?

_____

_____

_____

_____

_____

_____

_____

_____

Application: What one application will I put to use today or this weekend?

_____

_____

_____

MEDITATION 47

A man's pride will bring him low, but a humble spirit will obtain honor.

Proverbs 29:23

Trader's Paraphrase

A trader who believes that success is achieved by his abilities alone will be humiliated, but a trader who realizes he needs the help of God and others will be honored.

Notice the proverb says a humble *spirit* will obtain honor. Humility and pride are *spiritual* qualities. Your spirit has a profound effect on your trading. Your spirit can undermine or assist your natural thinking. Why spend months, even years, using only your mind to trade while ignoring the incredible capacity of your spirit? By all means, use your mind to develop your understanding of technical trading methods and the psychology of trading, but don't ignore the very center of your being, upon which your thinking is built.

Pride can cause you to ignore your own rules so that you indulge in trading by the seat of your pants (gambling). You, and those you love, cannot afford that indulgence. Pride can also cause you to dismiss the guidance of traders who are more successful than you. Pride makes it difficult to see your faults and other's knowledge. Why not personally test and use the proven guidelines of other traders? Humility has no problem honoring wisdom that originated from others. Of course, their methods and rules must apply to your trading style and market. Trading with humility increases your resources.

Paradoxically, if you are so concerned with maintaining a successful image that you do not let others see your trading mistakes or give you advice, you will be humbled by the very trading you were too proud to expose. But if you humble yourself, you will be honored because of your respect for others and your success.

RESPONSE 47

Response: What are my thoughts? What is God saying to me?

_____
_____
_____
_____
_____
_____
_____
_____

Brainstorming: What are 5 possible applications?

_____
_____
_____
_____
_____
_____
_____
_____

Application: What one application will I put to use today or this weekend?

_____
_____
_____
_____

MEDITATION 48

The horse is prepared for the day of battle, but victory belongs to the LORD.

Proverbs 21:31

Trader's Paraphrase

Even the most diligently prepared trader should realize that success comes from God.

Not only does humility precede honor, but humility after honor keeps your mind and heart in a proper perspective for continued success, including the smaller successes of a few good trades in a row or a few profitable trading days in a row. If you started relying on God to become successful in trading, and found that such an attitude of humility was a great benefit, then know that continued reliance on God will bring continued benefit. To drift from reliance on God to reliance on self, on others, on rules, or on methods, will pull you out of reliance on Wisdom and the fear of the Lord; it will leave you to your own limited devices.

This proverb may initially seem unusual, as it acknowledges that people made the preparations for battle, yet it gives credit to God for the victory. Isaiah 26:12 says something similar: *"…all that we have accomplished you have done for us"* (NIV). In ancient days, God told His people to fight some battles, while others He said He would fight for them. It was evident that either way the victorious outcome was from God. It is the same for you today.

Whether you trade by rules you developed over years of hard work, or by specific instructions from God for each trade, trading success comes from Him. Humility in trading, giving God honor in each trading victory, will keep your heart from drifting out of a healthy place spiritually and emotionally.

RESPONSE 48

Response: What are my thoughts? What is God saying to me?

_____
_____
_____
_____
_____
_____
_____
_____

Brainstorming: What are 5 possible applications?

_____
_____
_____
_____
_____
_____
_____

Application: What one application will I put to use today or this weekend?

_____
_____
_____
_____

MEDITATION 49

Pride goes before destruction, and a haughty spirit before stumbling.

Proverbs 16:18

Trader's Paraphrase

Believing that success is achieved by one's own abilities alone is destructive to trading, and an arrogant attitude leads to failure.

Why does destruction follow pride? Practically speaking, destruction is a logical effect of pride. Pride blinds you to things that are building up to destruction; you cannot turn things around if you don't see the need. Pride will not let you admit you need help. Pride causes you to reject help. Pride does not foresee adversity or put wise safety guards in place—why would you need them? Learning to succeed has two equally important sides; learning what works and learning what doesn't. Pride puts blind spots over things that are not being done right, creating an inability to address and change them.

There is a healthy, non-arrogant pride that comes from discovery and success; it comes from following your curiosity or need and finding or figuring out something. This healthy pride is a God-given source of satisfaction and joy. Humility enables you to acknowledge the same types of discoveries made by others and to benefit from what they have to offer.

Arrogant pride limits your ability to honor other people and their ideas, and it tends to reject beneficial information that didn't originate from you. Arrogant pride is not always a loud boisterous thing that can be easily recognized. Pride can be very quiet. Pride can be masked by false humility. Whether pride is expressed to others, or is kept quiet, it has the same destructive effect. Trading with humility will keep you from the stumbling caused by arrogance. It will allow you to see and avoid trouble that is building up to destruction.

RESPONSE 49

Response: What are my thoughts? What is God saying to me?

_____

_____

_____

_____

_____

_____

_____

_____

Brainstorming: What are 5 possible applications?

_____

_____

_____

_____

_____

_____

_____

_____

Application: What one application will I put to use today or this weekend?

_____

_____

_____

_____

MEDITATION 50

Everyone who is proud in heart is an abomination to the LORD; assuredly, he will not be unpunished.   Proverbs 16:5

Trader's Paraphrase

Every trader who believes that success is achieved by his abilities alone is detestable to God; he will surely be punished.

Most people are aware that a boastful kind of pride can be detrimental. But what is it that makes a proud heart actually "abominable" to God? Abominable is a strong word that isn't used much in our culture. We value tolerance so much that we may have forgotten that there is such a thing as an abomination. Some things are vile. There is such a thing as evil. But God has not lost perspective of what is real. So, again, what is so abominable, so despicable to God about a person who has a proud heart?

Love and relationships are of extreme importance to God. God is love, and He made us for love and relationship. Pride isolates and disconnects. Pride acts against relationships. A proud heart is what caused Lucifer's fall and expulsion from God's presence. A proud heart is what caused the human race's fall and expulsion from God's presence. A proud heart would do the same to you. Because pride creates distance between you and God, and between you and other people, it is an abomination of the worst kind to God.

To be a trader who is proud in heart causes you to ignore the wisdom God has made available in the book of Proverbs and in the rest of Scripture, to ignore the counsel of others, and to ignore what God shows you personally regarding your trading. A loving parent not only teaches his child what is good, but also warns against what will cause harm. God wants you to avoid the punishment that pride brings, and to know that a proud heart is an evil of the worst kind in His eyes.

RESPONSE 50

Response: What are my thoughts? What is God saying to me?

_____

_____

_____

_____

_____

_____

_____

_____

Brainstorming: What are 5 possible applications?

_____

_____

_____

_____

_____

_____

_____

_____

Application: What one application will I put to use today or this weekend?

_____

_____

_____

WEEKEND TEN
MEDITATION RESULTS

Improvements in My Thinking

_____
_____
_____
_____
_____
_____
_____
_____
_____
_____
_____

Improvements in My Trading

_____
_____
_____
_____
_____
_____
_____
_____
_____
_____
_____
_____
_____

WEEKEND TEN APPLICATION RESULTS

Day 46 Application Results

_____

_____

_____

_____

Day 47 Application Results

_____

_____

_____

_____

Day 48 Application Results

_____

_____

_____

_____

Day 49 Application Results

_____

_____

_____

_____

Day 50 Application Results

_____

_____

_____

_____

WEEK 11
TRADING WITH COMMUNITY

God has purposely designed you to have limited abilities and placed some of the help you need in others. Some of the trading wisdom you seek will only be found in community. Your personal trading resources may be well developed, but they are limited. Add several people to your pursuit of ongoing success in trading, and you have immediately multiplied your resources by those people you interact with. Why would you ever want to limit your trading to your own experience?

God said it is not good for people to be alone. You are designed to live and function in community. It is not good for you to be alone in your trading. Becoming part of a trading community may be the turning point in your success. You and others will be richly rewarded for your effort to join or form a community of like-minded traders.

MEDITATION 51

He who walks with wise men will be wise, but the companion of fools will suffer harm.   Proverbs 13:20

Trader's Paraphrase

The trader who associates with wise traders will be a wise trader, but the trader who associates with foolish traders will suffer for it.

What does it actually mean to walk with someone? The second half of the proverb uses an equivalent term: companion. When you walk with someone, you accompany them; you are their associate, their friend. You regularly share conversations, questions, answers, insights, and experiences. Things such as seminars, books, and audio and visual recordings from successful traders can bring immense benefit by allowing you to walk *behind* those traders. But that kind of indirect influence is very different from having a *relationship* that helps transform you into a wise and successful trader.

What a helpful bit of information—the people you associate with affect your level of wisdom. You can become a wise trader by seeking out and associating with wise traders!

Today's proverb says you will become like those you "walk" with. It may take a bit of history to determine if the people you are walking with are wise or foolish; a person's wisdom or foolishness is not always immediately apparent. Some people are wise in matters of trading but foolish in matters of the heart regarding untransformed affections and motivations for obtaining and using wealth. How tragic to be influenced by such people and to end up pursuing and using your wealth to the detriment of yourself and those you love. Trade in community with people who are wise in trading and wise in life; you will not only become a successful trader but a person who is wise in all areas of life.

RESPONSE 51

Response: What are my thoughts? What is God saying to me?

_____
_____
_____
_____
_____
_____
_____
_____

Brainstorming: What are 5 possible applications?

_____
_____
_____
_____
_____
_____
_____

Application: What one application will I put to use today or this weekend?

_____
_____
_____
_____

MEDITATION 52

Iron sharpens iron, so one man sharpens another.   Proverbs 27:17

Trader's Paraphrase

Iron sharpens iron, so one trader improves another.

We usually think of sharpening a metal tool with a harder or more abrasive substance. But today's proverb points out that just as iron can be used to sharpen iron—two implements made of the same material—so one trader can improve another. The most effective way to implement this proverb in your trading is to get a mentor or a peer trading partner to whom you are completely accountable; you should use whatever energy and resourcefulness is necessary to find one.

How is an iron tool or weapon sharpened? The thing that sharpens a tool or weapon made of metal is the same thing that sharpens you: pressure and abrasion are applied to shave off and make a new edge. The faults and failures of others do not necessarily disqualify them from being able to sharpen you, just as your faults do not disqualify you from being able to help them. Even if someone knows no more than you do about trading, they think and see differently than you. Suggestions, negative feedback, and other things you would rather people just kept to themselves may convey the very thing you need to hear.

As traders we rightfully look to those more experienced and successful than ourselves to sharpen our trading skills. But don't dismiss peer traders; they can also help sharpen you.

God loves to bless you directly, but He also likes to bless you indirectly through others. And He likes to bless others through you. Your breakthrough may be waiting for you in a close working relationship with a trading mentor or accountability partner; and your trading partner's breakthrough may be found in his relationship with you.

RESPONSE 52

Response: What are my thoughts? What is God saying to me?

_____
_____
_____
_____
_____
_____
_____
_____

Brainstorming: What are 5 possible applications?

_____
_____
_____
_____
_____
_____
_____
_____

Application: What one application will I put to use today or this weekend?

_____
_____
_____
_____

MEDITATION 53

Anxiety in a man's heart weighs it down, but a good word makes it glad.

Proverbs 12:25

Trader's Paraphrase

Anxiety handicaps a trader, but encouragement helps him.

In addition to the technical trading tips you can find in community, you can find help for your heart. If your heart is weighed down, so is your trading. Your computer, your books, your rules, your charts, and your indicators cannot discern when you are discouraged, nor can they choose to encourage you when you need it. It takes a live person to give you a good word that makes your anxious or discouraged heart glad again. You will find a constant source of encouragement in a community of like-minded traders.

Anxiety is debilitating to trading. It affects not only your trading but your whole life as well. You may be able to pull yourself out of anxiety on many occasions, but what about the times you are stuck for a while? Your trading will be off until your morale is lifted up.

And what about the part of you that is made to help others, to contribute, to encourage, to be a friend? Beside the encouragement you can *get* in community, you will also have the opportunity to *give* encouragement. You were created with the capacity to give, and so will have a sense of fulfillment as you make the time and use your opportunities to help others.

Few areas of your life function optimally when alone. The idea of being a lone ranger trader, with no one else to have to bother with or be accountable to, may have some appeal; but the negatives of trading alone outweigh the positives. Trading with the support of a community will make you more successful in trading and more fulfilled in life.

RESPONSE 53

Response: What are my thoughts? What is God saying to me?

_____

_____

_____

_____

_____

_____

_____

_____

Brainstorming: What are 5 possible applications?

_____

_____

_____

_____

_____

_____

_____

_____

Application: What one application will I put to use today or this weekend?

_____

_____

_____

_____

MEDITATION 54

The way of a fool is right in his own eyes, but a wise man is he who listens to counsel.   Proverbs 12:15

Trader's paraphrase

A foolish trader thinks he needs no help, but a wise trader listens to counsel.

A foolish trader is one who limits his trading to what seems right to him, and sees no need for input from other traders even if he keeps losing money. A foolish trader does not see himself as foolish, of course. So, how do you know if there is a bit of a foolish trader in you who is unwilling to listen to counsel? There are two ways not to listen to counsel: by actively dismissing counsel given or by passively not seeking it. Have you ever dismissed advice from successful traders and then paid the price? Are you currently dismissing guidelines from successful traders?

Although you can benefit greatly from indirectly submitting your trading to the counsel of trading books, seminars, and other methods of education, there is an additional level of insight that comes from person-to-person counsel. The interaction makes it harder to remain in denial, and you get the benefit of the minds, eyes, and experiences of others applied specifically to your trading. Trying to succeed without the help of others may seem appealing, but it limits your resources.

Trading as a *functioning* part of a trading community is a shortcut to gaining additional trading wisdom. If you regularly participate in a trading group, but never submit your trading for peer or mentor review, how will you get their trading counsel for your personal and specific trading methods? You may or may not agree with the counsel you get, but you won't know unless you listen. Don't let pride or inconvenience isolate you from finding or forming a community of like-minded traders.

RESPONSE 54

Response: What are my thoughts? What is God saying to me?

_____

_____

_____

_____

_____

_____

_____

_____

Brainstorming: What are 5 possible applications?

_____

_____

_____

_____

_____

_____

_____

Application: What one application will I put to use today or this weekend?

_____

_____

_____

_____

MEDITATION 55

A scoffer does not love one who reproves him, he will not go to the wise.

Proverbs 15:12

Trader's Paraphrase

A trader with a mocking attitude does not love a trader who points out his mistakes; he will not go to wise traders.

Do you love those people who point out areas of your trading that need improvement? When someone does point out a possible error in your trading methods, do you consider it or immediately scoff at it?

Scoffing is related to pride. To scoff is to belittle, put down, make fun of, discredit, or in some other way reject either the comments or the person who pointed out your need for improvement. Scoffing can be expressed or kept inside. No matter what drives a scoffing or belittling response, it robs you from rooting out self-defeating behaviors and causes you to avoid the very people who could help you.

Correction can benefit a wise listener, even if it is given out of a less-than-perfect motivation. People who are quick to point out other's mistakes may be difficult to listen to, but what they say may occasionally be worth something. You will have to decide if some people are too negative to be around or not. You do not have to allow someone with a critical spirit to speak into your life.

Others who have valuable insights may find it difficult to risk sharing them with you. If you criticize them for the help these people are trying to offer, you will shut them down and cheat yourself out of further counsel from them. Always thank people for their comments; doing so does not obligate you to do what they suggest. If you really see the value of reproof, you will appreciate the wisdom of having your faulty trading practices pointed out.

RESPONSE 55

Response: What are my thoughts? What is God saying to me?

_____
_____
_____
_____
_____
_____
_____
_____

Brainstorming: What are 5 possible applications?

_____
_____
_____
_____
_____
_____
_____
_____

Application: What one application will I put to use today or this weekend?

_____
_____
_____
_____

WEEKEND ELEVEN
MEDITATION RESULTS

Improvements in My Thinking

_____
_____
_____
_____
_____
_____
_____
_____
_____
_____
_____

Improvements in My Trading

_____
_____
_____
_____
_____
_____
_____
_____
_____
_____
_____
_____

WEEKEND ELEVEN
APPLICATION RESULTS

Day 51 Application Results

_____

_____

_____

_____

Day 52 Application Results

_____

_____

_____

_____

Day 53 Application Results

_____

_____

_____

_____

Day 54 Application Results

_____

_____

_____

_____

Day 55 Application Results

_____

_____

_____

_____

WEEK 12

TRADING WITH THE FEAR OF THE LORD

The book of Proverbs uses the phrase "the fear of the Lord" fifteen times and says the fear of the Lord is the beginning of wisdom. But why would you be afraid of a God of love? If you are afraid of the Lord, how can you live and work in a healthy relationship with Him?

The seemingly incongruent idea of fearing God, who is the source of all love, may be the reason behind the tradition of some Bible teachers and translators using the English word *reverence* rather than fear; they talk about reverencing the Lord not fearing Him. But in softening the Scriptural word *fear* to the word *reverence*, in an effort to communicate the understanding of some teachers and translators, I believe we are somewhat hindered from a view and attitude toward God that is absolutely foundational for gaining wisdom. So, let's examine the fear of the Lord further.

A helpful paraphrase that communicates a vital component of the fear of the Lord to our current cultural understanding, and which keeps the plain meaning of the original biblical language, is: *the fear of displeasing God.* This type of fear keeps you from harm, like the fear of misusing electricity. Sometimes an opposite phrase helps give understanding to the original phrase. Scripture uses such a phrase to describe a fear that does lead to harm: *"The fear of man brings a snare"* (Proverbs 29:25). It makes no sense to understand this as *reverence* for people. But when you understand it as *the fear of displeasing people,* it makes sense.

The motivation behind being afraid to displease either God or a person has two sides: the fear of *getting* negative consequences and the fear of *losing* beneficial consequences. If you don't see someone as having the power to harm or help you, you likely won't be afraid of displeasing him or her. God has the final say and ultimate power to bring you love, protection, justice, and blessings, or to let you reap devastation. People do not have that ultimate power over you. When you honor God by choosing not to displease him in your trading, your heart becomes teachable and open to the highest and purest source of trading wisdom.

MEDITATION 56

The fear of the Lord *is the beginning of knowledge.*   Proverbs 1:7

The fear of the Lord *is the beginning of wisdom.*   Proverbs 9:10

Trader's Paraphrase

The fear of displeasing God is the beginning of knowledge for trading.

The fear of displeasing God is the beginning of wisdom for trading.

There is a tendency to categorize God as the expert in "spiritual" matters and humans as experts in "practical" areas, such as trading. First Kings 10:23 says that King Solomon was the richest man in all the earth. Part of his wealth came from trading (not quite what we are referring to as "trading" in this book, but trading none the less). He was the head of national and international trading ventures. Influential people from all over the world traveled to hear his wisdom and see the wealth his wisdom produced. The most business savvy investor and trader in the ancient world said that knowledge and wisdom begin with the fear of the Lord, including the nut-and-bolts financial knowledge and wisdom that made him the world's richest man for several decades.

Since the fear of the Lord is the beginning, the foundation, the gate to wisdom and knowledge for trading, you must start there. You don't want to build your trading on an inferior foundation, only to have it shift and sink later. God has given us teachers to help dispense His knowledge and wisdom. But don't allow your heart or your mind to put more confidence in books, instructors, coaches, trading systems, trading software, or anything other than the One who has all financial market knowledge and the wisdom to apply it.

If you want to acquire superior knowledge and wisdom for sustained success in trading, begin with a complete and constant deference to God as you trade and study trading.

RESPONSE 56

Response: What are my thoughts? What is God saying to me?

_____

_____

_____

_____

_____

_____

_____

_____

Brainstorming: What are 5 possible applications?

_____

_____

_____

_____

_____

_____

_____

_____

Application: What one application will I put to use today or this weekend?

_____

_____

_____

MEDITATION 57

My son, if you will receive my words and treasure my commandments within you, make your ear attentive to wisdom, incline your heart to understanding; for if you cry for discernment, lift your voice for understanding; if you seek her as silver and search for her as for hidden treasures; then you will discern the fear of the LORD and discover the knowledge of God. For the LORD gives wisdom; from His mouth come knowledge and understanding.   Proverbs 2:1-6

Trader's paraphrase

Tune your ears to listen for trading wisdom, and let your heart treat that wisdom as a treasure; for if you seek trading wisdom as if you were searching for buried treasure, you will see the benefit of the fear of displeasing God, and you will come to know God. For it is God who gives wisdom to trade, and from his mouth comes knowledge and understanding to trade.

If you knew the location of buried treasure so great that gold or diamonds didn't even compare, how much effort would you spend to obtain it? Wisdom can make you prosper—not only financially, but in every area in life. Your effort to do anything in life should automatically include gaining the wisdom to make that effort succeed.

Notice the proverb says wisdom comes from God. He put together and maintains everything in the physical and spiritual world, so He is the One who understands how everything works. You can and should get trading wisdom through people who have some. But since God is the source of all wisdom, and since He made you for relationship and fellowship with Him, He also wants to give trading wisdom to you directly and to fellowship with you as you trade. If you want wisdom as you are analyzing your trades, fear the Lord and fellowship with Him while you analyze your trades. If you want wisdom in the moment of trading, fear the Lord and fellowship with Him while you trade.

RESPONSE 57

Response: What are my thoughts? What is God saying to me?

_____

_____

_____

_____

_____

_____

_____

_____

_____

Brainstorming: What are 5 possible applications?

_____

_____

_____

_____

_____

_____

_____

_____

_____

Application: What one application will I put to use today or this weekend?

_____

_____

_____

_____

MEDITATION 58

In the fear of the LORD there is strong confidence, and his children will have refuge.

Proverbs 14:26

Trader's Paraphrase

The trader who fears displeasing God will trade with strong confidence, and his children will have a refuge.

The fear of the Lord will give you confidence in trading. If you fear displeasing Him while you trade, you will not only have confidence but *strong* confidence. Trading with confidence comes in part through time and experience, and through things like extensive back testing and paper trading, knowing each trading system's percentages, mastering trading by your rules, and excelling in knowing the personalities of the specific markets you trade and the indicators you use. But there is a deeper confidence at the heart level that comes from fearing the Lord. Nothing shakes God. If you fear displeasing Him, nothing will shake you.

Something wonderful happens when you are operating in the fear of the Lord; things like fear and pride are displaced. He speaks things that you would otherwise not hear or be able to receive. He counsels you. He turns on a river of wisdom for you and puts you in it.

There is a second, priceless benefit to the fear of the Lord. It creates a place of refuge, a shelter from the storms of life, for your children. Your "children" includes not only your natural children but also those you mentor or teach, those you have influence over. As is the case with so many other good choices, choosing to remain in the fear of the Lord benefits both yourself and those you love and care for. Fearing to displease the Lord positions you to trade in the presence and Wisdom of God and creates a place of refuge, a place of spiritual protection for your children and for those you influence.

RESPONSE 58

Response: What are my thoughts? What is God saying to me?

_____

_____

_____

_____

_____

_____

_____

_____

_____

Brainstorming: What are 5 possible applications?

_____

_____

_____

_____

_____

_____

_____

_____

Application: What one application will I put to use today or this weekend?

_____

_____

_____

_____

MEDITATION 59

The fear of man brings a snare, but he who trusts in the Lord *will be exalted.*

Proverbs 29:25

Trader's Paraphrase

The fear of displeasing people in trading is a trap, but he who trusts in God will have trading success.

If you fear people's opinion of you, if you are a people pleaser, and if you are trying to be approved or honored in the eyes of people, you are walking into a snare; you are heading towards being captured or entangled. That snare can keep you from advancing and obtaining blessing, success, and honor. But if you trust in God, if you have high regard for His opinion of you, and if you are trying to please him, you will be exalted, approved, and honored. You cannot fear displeasing man and displeasing God at the same time. Further, be aware that even if you fear God in general, there may still be limited areas in which you fear man. If you can identify a limited area in which you fear man, you have identified a fear that can be eliminated, so God can exalt you.

How would you apply this to trading? If you choose or default to seeking approval from people, one snare is the inability to show your trading to fellow traders or to a mentor, resulting in the loss of whatever wisdom they may have for you. They may be able to uncover and root up bad trading habits in you and help establish some good habits in you instead. The fear of losing other people's approval can be a trap that keeps you from acting in your best interest.

Take a risk. Stretch yourself. Let go of the fear of man, and show your trades to a trusted fellow trader or mentor. Look to your Creator Father for approval. Fearing God, and not fearing man, will help you avoid trading snares; and the Lord will exalt you in trading.

RESPONSE 59

Response: What are my thoughts? What is God saying to me?

_____

_____

_____

_____

_____

_____

_____

_____

Brainstorming: What are 5 possible applications?

_____

_____

_____

_____

_____

_____

_____

_____

Application: What one application will I put to use today or this weekend?

_____

_____

_____

MEDITATION 60

Because I called and you refused, I stretched out my hand and no one paid attention; and you neglected all my counsel and did not want my reproof; I will also laugh at your calamity; I will mock when your dread comes, when your dread comes like a storm and your calamity comes like a whirlwind, when distress and anguish come upon you. Then they will call on me, but I will not answer; they will seek me diligently but they will not find me, because they hated knowledge and did not choose the fear of the Lord. They would not accept my counsel, they spurned all my reproof. So they shall eat of the fruit of their own way and be satiated with their own devices. Proverbs 1:24-31

Trader's Paraphrase

If you neglect the trading counsel God offers you and have no fear of displeasing Him, He will neglect the disastrous results of trading your own way.

Since God is love, He calls to warn and offers His counsel to spare people from disastrous results. But once you choose, God will honor your choices. Notice that God is not causing the storm of calamity, dread, distress, or anguish. The proverb says these things are the fruit of choosing one's own way. Notice also that you must *choose* the fear of the Lord. This choice is not necessarily automatic because you believe in God or have committed your life to Him.

It may take some training and practice to establish the habit of trading in the fear of the Lord, but you can do it. Another more intimate approach is to focus on trading without breaking your fellowship with God. Talk with Him about what you are seeing and ask what He is seeing, listen for His counsel, follow that counsel, and honor the rules you have developed with His help. If you were trading in fellowship with God, you would have to break that fellowship and revert to doing things your own way to step out of the fear of the Lord.

RESPONSE 60

Response: What are my thoughts? What is God saying to me?

_____
_____
_____
_____
_____
_____
_____
_____
_____

Brainstorming: What are 5 possible applications?

_____
_____
_____
_____
_____
_____
_____
_____
_____

Application: What one application will I put to use today or this weekend?

_____
_____
_____
_____

WEEKEND TWELVE MEDITATION RESULTS

Improvements in My Thinking

_____

_____

_____

_____

_____

_____

_____

_____

_____

_____

Improvements in My Trading

_____

_____

_____

_____

_____

_____

_____

_____

_____

_____

WEEKEND TWELVE
APPLICATION RESULTS

Day 56 Application Results

Day 57 Application Results

Day 58 Application Results

Day 59 Application Results

Day 60 Application Results

YOUR PROGRESS THIS QUARTER

Review and summarize your improvement this quarter, using the following pages.

Note: You may want to go though the course several times, to reinforce your progress and establish your trading using your new spiritual resources. If you want to have a fresh workbook be sure to order your next copy in time, especially if you are working through it as part of a group (highly recommended!).

You can find additional resources at proverbsfortraders.com

YOUR PROGRESS THIS QUARTER

Significant improvements in my thinking the past three months

YOUR PROGRESS
THIS QUARTER

Significant improvements in my trading the past three months

_____

_____

_____

_____

_____

_____

_____

_____

_____

_____

_____

_____

_____

_____

_____

_____

_____

_____

_____

_____

_____

_____

_____

_____

PART 2

RISING ABOVE THE AMATEUR LEVEL

PART 2 INTRODUCTION

Rules

Many amateur traders will not keep rules. They are not diligent in developing and keeping their own trading rules, nor will they adopt and keep rules developed by others. Working through Parts 1 and 3 of this book will help you develop the ability to keep rules.

Money Management

Many amateur traders will not use prudent money management practices. They risk too much per trade and per month, and they continue trading without stopping to make changes when their account has lost a significant percentage. Applying the following Industry Standards for Money Management will help you preserve your trading capital so you can go on to become a profitable trader.

Trading System

Many amateur traders will not complete the trading system development process. They will not fully develop their own system, nor will they adequately test a system that has been developed by others. Using the following Trading System Development guidelines will help you avoid years of frustration and go on to become a successful trader.

INDUSTRY STANDARDS FOR MONEY MANAGEMENT

The following industry standards for risk and account management come from years of professional experience. Risking beyond these limits creates a slippery slope toward irrecoverable losses. Trading without predetermining how much you are willing to lose before you will halt trading is very foolish. It is prudent to commit to loss limits on each trade, each month, and each trading account before you put any money at risk. Unlimited risk positions you for unlimited loss, but limiting your risk gives you the opportunity to stay in the game and learn how to make consistent gains. Have you already set and do you act on predetermined loss limits for every trade, every month, and every account?

You must also have trading capital before you trade. Some people dismiss the wisdom in trading only money not needed for living or other expenses. Risking only what money you and your family can get by without is acting in wisdom. Many desperate people will ignore this advice, thinking the opportunity outweighs the risk—it does not. Please don't be one of those people.

Here are summarized recommendations from top-level trading experts. The percentages below relate to total capital in your account. You will notice that some advise risking more than others. We will discuss that afterwards.

Edwards, Magee & Bassetti, in their book *Technical Analysis of Stock Trends*[1]
- ♦ For the first *two years* of learning, most of your trading should be paper trading; you should use only a small amount of your actual capital, and you should not depend on taking any withdrawals.

- ♦ Don't risk money that is not trading capital; don't risk living expenses.

- ♦ Don't risk more than you can lose with only a small discomfort.

- ♦ Maximum risk per trade: 2-3%.

Kirkpatrick & Dahlquist, in their book *Technical Analysis*[2]
- ♦ Maximum risk and loss per trade: 2% (the difference between entry price and stop price)

- ♦ Trading should stop completely for re-evaluation if an account loses 20%

Dr. Alexander Elder, in his book *Trading for a Living*[3]

💎 Maximum risk per trade: 1-2% (including commissions and slippage)

💎 Maximum risk per month: 6-8%

John J. Murphy, in his book *Technical Analysis of the Financial Markets*[4]

The following guidelines are for futures trading, but may be useful for other trading.

💎 Total margin held for simultaneous positions: 50% maximum

💎 Total margin held in related markets: 20-25% maximum

💎 Total margin held in one market: 10-15% maximum

💎 Total risk [not the margin held, but the difference between entry and stop] for a single trade: 5% maximum

The maximum recommended risk for a single trade varied from expert to expert: 1-2%; 2%; 2-3%; and 5%. So, which should you choose? Keeping in mind that the reason for risk management is to survive a series of losing trades and preserve capital, one method is presented in the following pages. (We are talking here about the amount of *risk*, the difference between entry and stop, including commissions and slippage. We are not addressing here the larger amount of *margin* used for futures and options.)

There are at least three areas for which you need predetermined loss limits.

1. Total account risk
2. Monthly risk
3. Risk per trade for each different system

Total Account Risk

First, decide how much of your total account are you willing to lose before you will halt trading to analyze and make changes so your account balance stops declining. Many successful traders use Kirkpatrick and Dahlquist's limit of 20% on a declining account balance as a point to stop trading. The 20% figure gives you a reasonable drawdown margin for months that do not work well with your system(s) but also gives you a reality check and a way to preserve the majority of your trading capital. If you are not financially or emotionally able to handle a loss of 20% of your trading account, risk less.

From which point in time should this 20% be calculated? If your account balance is currently below its opening value, use the opening amount to protect your initial capital. If your account balance is or was above its opening balance, use the account's highest balance to protect your profits. If you have already lost more than 20% of your beginning or highest balance, stop trading immediately to preserve what beginning capital or profits are left; work through the trade development process (see next chapter) before risking money again.

If you have not already done so, why not decide now how much of your account you are financially and emotionally prepared to lose and implement your overall account stop loss. If your account balance is increasing, also decide how often you will recalculate your total account loss limit. Figure the limit as a dollar (or other currency) amount, rather than just as a percentage, so you will realize when you are getting close.

The percent of my account I am prepared to lose: _____

The account's highest balance: _____

The account's current balance: _____

Current percent of loss from highest balance: _____

Remaining *percent* of account available for risk: _____

Remaining *money amount* available for risk: _____

I will recalculate every (time period or profit amount/percent) _____

Monthly Risk

Next, decide how many months of consecutive loss you want your account to be able to survive and divide that number into the total account percent you decided to risk. This will give you the percent of your account you would be willing to lose before you stop trading for the month. Let's say you want to be able to survive three consecutive months of loss, and are financially and emotionally able to handle a loss of 20% of your account. You would arrive at your maximum monthly risk of loss in the following way:

Twenty percent of your account balance divided by 3 months equals 6.66%. Let's lower that to 6 percent to simplify our following examples and to give ourselves a little margin of safety for surviving three full months of consecutive loss, should it occur. So the amount you would be prepared to lose, the percent of your account you would risk monthly, would be 6%. This fits within Dr. Elder's recommended limit of 6-8 percent. If you trade only one system, you could risk the whole 6% on that system. If you trade more than one system, you may want to divide the monthly risk among your systems, so you could continue trading each system throughout the month.

For example, if you have three systems, maybe you would risk 2% per system monthly, or maybe you wish to divide the risk in a different manner. The reduction for multiple systems would allow you to continue trading the profitable systems while halting the system(s) that are not working well with the market conditions in a given month. Alternately, you could risk the full 6% on each system, and then stop trading *all* systems for the month if their combined loss reaches the 6% limit.

Whether you allow the full monthly risk for each system, or divide the amount you are prepared to lose monthly into multiple systems, you must stop trading when the risk of *the next trade* would take you over your predetermined monthly risk. Stop trading each losing system for the rest of the month, preserve your trading capital, and spend the rest of the month analyzing your records and paper trading or back testing.

If you have not already done so, why not decide how many months of consecutive loss you want your account to be able to survive, and set your monthly loss limit now.

I want my account to survive _____ consecutive months of trading loss. Those number of months divided into the total percent of my account I am willing to risk (lose) gives me a monthly loss limit of _____ percent, and a dollar (or other currency) amount of _____ (based on today's account balance).

Risk per Trade for each System

Calculating your risk per trade, figured specifically for each trading system, will help you determine two things: 1) if you have enough trading capital to trade yet and 2) how much to risk per trade to be able to survive a string of losing trades while staying within your monthly loss limit. We are not talking here about the amount that is risked using the initial stop required by each system, but rather how much money to allocate to each trade; the maximum number of contracts, options, or stocks you should risk per trade for each trading system you use. This step begins after you have completed the back testing and paper trading steps of trade development (see the next chapter) and before you begin trading with money.

First, calculate each system's largest drawdown, using the smallest amount your market and system will allow (one contract, one stock, etc.). Use the total loss amount produced by the longest string of losing trades for each system (your month may start at or near the beginning of a losing streak). Alternately, you could just set an amount at which you will stop trading (this may be helpful for systems that have occasional months with large losses, but are otherwise profitable).

If you have not already done so, why not calculate the largest monthly drawdown for each of your trading systems.

Name of system: _____ Largest drawdown: _____
Name of system: _____ Largest drawdown: _____
Name of system: _____ Largest drawdown: _____

Next, compare your largest drawdown with your monthly risk limit. **This is the most important step in this chapter, and possibly the most important consideration in your money management.** If your systems' combined largest drawdown is *more* than your monthly risk limit, you must make adjustments: find a market or systems that will allow you to trade with less money or get more trading capital. Unless God is giving you trade-by-trade guidance (He does with some people) *trading without sufficient funds is gambling. Trading without a fully developed system is also gambling.* I urge you not to gamble with your God-given trading capital. Trading capital is money you don't need for living or other expenses. God is able to fund His will according to His timing. Will you choose to *trust* Him in this area and prosper, even if it takes much longer than you anticipated, or will you trade in haste and gamble your money away?

If your systems' combined drawdown is *less* than your monthly risk limit, you can increase the amount you risk per trade. Before risking the full amount your account and risk limits will allow, always begin trading a new system with the *smallest amount* each system and will allow. Trading with money produces different results than paper trading, due to slippage and order fills, as well as the emotional and physiological impact. Increase the amount you trade with *gradually,* as you build a history of discipline and confidence trading each system.

Here is a table giving an example of how much to risk per trade. Some lines are not realistic (such as expecting only one loss in a row), but it demonstrates the concept. This table limits losses to 6% per month to survive 3 consecutive losing months without your account losing more than 20%. The table is built on a single system's *longest string* of losses. (If you use more than one system, you must consider the combined impact.)

      1 losing trade in a row: you could risk up to 6% per trade

      2 losing trades in a row: you could risk up to 3% per trade

      3 losing trades in a row: you could risk up to 2% per trade

      4 losing trades in a row: you could risk up to 1.5% per trade

      5 losing trades in a row: you could risk up to 1.2% per trade

      6 losing trades in a row: you could risk up to 1% per trade

More than 6 losing trades in a row: divide 6% by the number of losing trades

Do you see the significance of basing your risk per trade on each system's longest string of consecutive losing trades, rather than just arbitrarily choosing to risk 5% or even 1%? You don't want to get taken out of the game by risking more per trade than is prudent for *your systems*. If you have not already done so, why not calculate now the maximum risk per trade for each of your trading systems. (Remember, if you use more than one system, you may want to consider the impact of their combined risk.) Figure the risk as a percent of your account and as a specific amount of money. If you have a large account, these amounts will be larger than the largest drawdown figures from the previous page.

System: _____ Risk percent _____ Risk amount _____

System: _____ Risk percent _____ Risk amount _____

System: _____ Risk percent _____ Risk amount _____

With changes in markets, systems, and account balances, you will need to recalculate your maximum risk per trade. When will you recalculate?

I will recalculate risk per trade every (day; week; month) _____

There are certainly other methods of risk management. The previous pages are only one approach. But whatever method you use, you need limits on total account, monthly risk, and risk per trade for each trading system. Some traders, such as very active day traders, need a daily loss limit as well. If your account size is too small to stay within reasonable risk limits, you don't have enough money to trade yet. Either find a system or a market that will allow you to risk less or get more trading capital. Haste will wipe out your trading account. Even if you have a desperate need to make money, and trading seems to be your only option, those are not reasons for allowing yourself to trade foolishly.

Amateurs tend to focus on what they could make, and continue trading without setting or keeping loss limits. Professionals are willing to stop trading when their limits are hit.

TRADING SYSTEM DEVELOPMENT

If you enter a trade that is not supported by a fully developed or fully adopted trading system, you are gambling. The essence of gambling is betting on an uncertain outcome. If you have not defined, tested, and calculated the averaged results of the trade you are about to enter, you are betting on an uncertain outcome. Although the outcome of any single trade is uncertain, there is a reasonable basis for expecting an averaged outcome on a certain number of trades based on strict adherence to tested rules under specific conditions. Even years of experience alone are not sufficient for risking trading capital without completing the trading system development process. Do not allow the devastation of your trading capital by tolerating denial—trading without a fully developed system is gambling.

Although many of us expected to become successful traders soon after purchasing an educational course or a program that automatically generates entry and exit signals, the unadvertised reality is that even diligent traders often need *at least* a couple of years to learn technical trading methods and develop or adopt a trading system. The time needed for learning and system development will also apply to some extent for every *new* method of trading, such as changing between investing, swing trading, or day trading or when changing between trading stocks, options, currencies, or futures.

A fuller description of the trade development process is outside the scope of this book, and may be found in other books, including some of those listed in the Bibliography. What I want to accomplish here is to concisely spell out critical steps at the heart of the process for use in this book as a guide and checklist. These steps are a practical application of Proverbs 21:5, "The plans of the diligent lead surely to abundance, but everyone who is hasty comes only to poverty" (ESV).

Before you are ready to build a system, you must consider and decide on several things. Let's take a look.

Three Types of Trading Systems
- Nondiscretionary (mechanical/automated)
- Partial discretionary (trader acts on automatically generated entry and/or exit signals)
- Discretionary (trader makes all choices based on experience)

If you have already learned the methods of technical trading and you have or can get access to auto-mated back testing and trading, by all means use it. Automated back testing will eliminate months of work compared to manual back testing. Fully automated, nondiscretionary trading removes the emotional components that so often sabotage discretionary trading, and in that respect it is a superior way of trading. Even if your trading is fully automated, whether the system was developed by you or by someone else, you should still complete steps 5-12 of The Trading System Development Process.

The Components of a Complete System (Faith, *The Original Turtle Trading Rules*)[5]

A Complete Trading System covers each of the decisions required for successful trading:

- Markets—What to buy or sell

- Position Sizing—How much to buy or sell

- Entries—When to buy or sell

- Stops—When to get out of a losing position

- Exits—When to get out of a winning position

- Tactics—How to buy or sell [how orders are placed]

What is a Good Trading System? (Kirkpatrick & Dahlquist, *Technical Analysis*)[6]

- Has a small number of robust trading rules (less than ten each for entry and exit)

- Can be used in multiple markets by adjusting the parameters while keeping the same rules

- Limits risk to a 20% drawdown

- Is fully mechanical, eliminating second-guessing while trading

Additional Decisions

- Will I trade longer trends, swing trade, or scalp? How long will my trades last: days, hours, or minutes?

- What days and hours will I trade? Am I a morning or a night person? Which days and times are most profitable for my chosen markets?

- Will I hold positions overnight? Over the weekend?

- Will I trade trends, counter trends, turns, channels, patterns, other?

Having looked at all that came before in this chapter, here is the heart of what I wanted you to have. Here are the main components and the order of developing a trading system. Following and completing the process will give you a solid guide and help you avoid losing money due to trading before you were adequately prepared.

The Trading System Development Process

1. **Create initial rules** for a way of trading you think has potential.
2. **Back test** rules on historical charts, keeping an *extremely detailed* record of the trade and **the results.**
3. **Analyze** results and adjust rules or abandon strategy.
4. **Repeat back testing steps 2 & 3 until results are satisfactory.**
5. **Paper trade** in live or replayed market, keeping an *extremely detailed* record of the trade and the results.
6. **Analyze** results and adjust rules or abandon strategy.
7. **Repeat paper trading steps 5 & 6 until results are satisfactory.**
8. **Test trade by risking a *very small percent of your account,*** (See the chapter on Money Management for guidelines) keeping an *extremely detailed* record of the trade and the results.
9. **Analyze** results and adjust rules or abandon strategy.
10. **Repeat** back testing and paper trading steps as necessary before trading again with a ***very small amount*** of money until results are satisfactory.
11. **Gradually** increase money and contracts used for trades, within money management limits, when results are satisfactory at each stage.
12. **Continue** keeping *extremely detailed* records of the trade and the results, analyzing, and if necessary, adjusting rules—for as long as you use the system.

Murphy, in *Technical Analysis of the Financial Markets*, says that less than 5 percent of ideas for a trading system usually end up back testing successfully, and most of those will not end up successful in the transition to actual trading.[7] So don't be discouraged if you have to take many ideas through the trade development process before coming up with a successful one; you are right on track. Focus on the rewards of producing a successful system and let your vision for the five areas covered in Week Three encourage you.

Short circuiting the system development steps will short circuit your progress to profitable trading. Be patient. It will take as long as it takes. Even if you have a pressing need or a passionate vision for additional income, put in all the time and effort necessary to complete the steps. Haste will prolong your access to wealth. Remember that, *"Wealth gained hastily will dwindle, but whoever gathers **little by little** will increase it."* Proverbs 13:11 (ESV)

Action Steps

Use the rest of this page and the next to record the actions you want to take in response to this chapter. Assign a tentative date to accomplish each step. Make a copy and post the dates on your calendar as a reminder.

_____

_____

_____

_____

_____

Action Steps (continued)

PART 3

EQUIPPING YOUR SPIRIT FOR SUCCESS

PART 3 INTRODUCTION

In this section, you will gain resources for identifying and breaking connection with any demonic influences that have been limiting or controlling your trading; you will learn how to gain new *spiritual* trading tools; and finally, since the Spirit of Wisdom is spiritual and can only be received by those whose spirits have been born again, you will have the opportunity to be born again as a spiritual child of God.

An important note: In order to apply what you read in Freedom from Demonic Influences, you must be born again spiritually, not only to receive the Spirit of Wisdom, but to have spiritual authority to obtain your spiritual freedom. Colossians 1:13 says, *"For He* [God, the Father] *rescued us* [God's spiritual children] *from the domain of darkness, and transferred us to the kingdom of His beloved Son."* By default we are all under the influence of Satan's kingdom of darkness; Jesus said Satan is the prince of this world (John 12:31 and 16:11). You cannot break connection with destructive spiritual influences until you have been transferred out from Satan's demonic kingdom of darkness and into Jesus' Kingdom of light. So, if you are not sure if you are spiritually born again yet, please work through the Maximizing Wisdom section before attempting to apply what is taught in Freedom from Demonic Influences in Trading.

An additional note: many who have been born again have done so with a limited understanding and therefore limited transformation, because of the Church's lack of emphasis on Jesus' two main calls (see Maximizing Wisdom), and consequently have not been able to make a clean break with this world or their old life. Basically, everyone should go through Maximizing Wisdom to either become a spiritual child of God and start living as a disciple of Jesus in the Kingdom of God (rather than just as a "Christian."), or to see if you can add to your understanding to help others in their spiritual life.

FREEDOM FROM DEMONIC INFLUENCES IN TRADING

In Part 1, you dealt with issues of the heart that affect your trading. You unpacked and applied wisdom to succeed financially in such a way that brings blessing instead of ruin. In this section, you will gain personal victory over demonic spirits that have been allowed tremendous influence in the financial markets and that can gain a stronghold of influence over individuals to sabotage trading success. You will learn how God can help you identify these destructive spiritual influences, break any hold they have on you, and obtain righteous, grace-empowered spiritual trading tools. Then you will go on to establish strongholds of righteousness in your trading, which will bring blessings to your life and to the lives of those you influence.

Demonic Influences in the Financial Markets

As we mentioned in day thirteen's meditation, people can release destructive, unrighteous spirits into their sphere of influence, such as the financial markets, by acting in agreement with them. Additionally, mankind has abdicated his righteous rule over this earth through making unrighteous choices, and Satan and his kingdom of darkness have gained temporary rule over the earth (See John 12:31). So demonic spirits that inspire the love of money, greed, fear, unethical practices, and so on have been allowed to operate in the financial markets. Traders functioning in such a demonically influenced area can unknowingly be influenced, or even controlled, by those spirits.

Can a Christian's Trading be Affected by Demons?

Some Christians assume demons can never gain power over us, since God has delivered us from the kingdom of darkness and transferred us into His Kingdom. But what if we do not exercise our authority over darkness? What if instead of actively resisting demonic influences, we passively tolerate or come into agreement with them? Let's consider a Scripture that instructs us about the potential influence demonic spirits could gain in a Christian's life.

Ephesians 4:26-27 (NIV) says, *"'In your anger do not sin': Do not let the sun go down while you are still angry, and **do not give** the devil a foothold."* Anger can originate as a normal and appropriate response to things such as violation of personal boundaries, injustice, pain, or fear. This verse, written to Christians, shows that you can *give* the devil (or his demonic, fallen angel associates) a foothold within you if you *allow* anger to lead you into sin or *allow* anger to remain unaddressed.

Agreement with anger, intentional or unintentional, can give a spirit of anger permission to establish a foothold, a stronghold, within you. Just as failing to deal with anger in a righteous manner can lead to a demonic stronghold, failing to live in a righteous manner in other areas can also lead to the establishment of other demonic strongholds within us.

The Bible contains verses mentioning specific spirits, including a spirit of fear, a spirit of confusion, a spirit of slavery, and a spirit of jealousy, as well as a spirit of self-discipline, a spirit of knowledge, a spirit of faith, a spirit of truth, and many more. Some scriptural uses of the term "a spirit of…" seem to describe a human *attitude*, while some clearly describe a *demonic* or *angelic* spirit with a special assignment. But Scripture does not give a specific all-inclusive list of demonic spirits. So if your trading seems to be influenced or even controlled by some self-defeating or destructive impulse, keep reading.

Understanding the psychology of trading is tremendous for dealing with things that hinder us from successful trading on a *natural* level. Some obstacles to success however are not natural but spiritual. Spiritual obstacles must be dealt with on a *spiritual* level. And oppression by demonic spirits must be dealt with spiritually. Later in this section, you will learn how to use your spiritual authority in Jesus to obtain the freedom He already won for you.

If you are not pro-active, if you do not exert God's grace-empowered spiritual effort, you may default to agreement with destructive, ungodly, demonic influences. For example, you do not have to declare, "I hereby come into agreement with the spirit of fear," in order to come into agreement with the spirit of fear and give it permission to influence you. Coming into agreement with the spirit of fear can happen by harboring a fearful thought, acting on a fear-driven compulsion, indulging a feeling of fear, or tolerating a fearful motivation. The same applies to any unrighteous spirit; by coming into agreement with it, we open a door and we allow it to influence our lives.

So, whether destructive thoughts, choices, feelings, or motivations originate from you or from an unrighteous spirit, you can and must use your authority in Christ to actively disallow them, or you may end up passively allowing them to remain and gain a position of influence or control over you. *"Submit therefore to God. Resist the devil and he **will** flee from you"* (James 4:7). As a spiritual child of God, when you continue to resist ungodly spirits, they cannot gain a hold on you, and sooner or later they will leave.

Is Your Trading Affected by Demonic Influences?

If you have not been able to get breakthrough to profitable trading after several years of diligent effort, consider the *possibility* that you may have unknowingly opened a door to demonic influences. Do you have self-defeating habits that you cannot break? Do you have trading related addictions, or do you have non-trading related addictions which affect your mental or emotional capacity to trade, or which consume your trading capital?

The apostle Paul had this to say about overwhelming, unrighteous, destructive, addictive habits: *"Do you not know that when you present yourselves to someone as slaves for obedience, you are slaves of the one whom you obey, either of sin resulting in death, or of obedience resulting in righteousness?"* (Romans 6:16) Paul is speaking about spiritual addictions: slavery to sin. When you obey, when you come into agreement with either sin or righteousness, you end up becoming a slave to it.

Let's look at a few common demonically influenced trading strongholds. Do you think your trading is being affected by any of them?

Gambling

The spirit of gambling is common in the financial markets, yet many traders are not aware that they are influenced by it. The tricky thing about recognizing the spirit of gambling is that its *compulsion* can co-exist with a righteous *passion* to make money in trading. There are some of you that have a call on your life to produce wealth through trading to help those in need or to support the health and growth of God's Kingdom on earth. A spirit of gambling can sabotage your call to produce wealth through trading, until you recognize and root it out.

The spirit of gambling produces an overwhelming urge to bet on an uncertain outcome and is based on the belief that you can make money in a small amount of time without building wealth prudently. Gambling releases an addictive rush of excitement that provides momentary escape from emotional pain, depression, and responsibility. Gambling blinds a person to its true cost and exaggerates its benefits.

When we come into agreement with an urge to make money by betting on an uncertain outcome, we open the door for a spirit of gambling. If you have overwhelming urges to bet on uncertain outcomes, whether in a game of chance, in a sport, or in trading, the spirit of gambling probably has a stronghold in you, and you will need deliverance from it. Deliverance is being set free from the control of a demonic spirit by the authority of the Kingdom of God. We will look into deliverance later in this section.

Do you identify with any of these trading gambling statements?

- ❖ I've seen this setup work before so this is not gambling, even though I don't know the statistical outcomes for this specific setup.

- ❖ I continue to take trades outside of fully developed trading systems, even though I continue to lose money.

- ❖ I continue trading to make money, even though my account balance declines month after month.

Overtrading

Overtrading, as we are addressing it here, is continuing to trade when you are out of control. If you have worked through what is offered by experts in the psychology of trading, and you still cannot stop overtrading, you may have opened the door to a demonic spirit that has gained influence or control over you. Do you identify with any of these overtrading statements?

- ❖ I can't stop trading until I get my money back

- ❖ I just made all my money back, so why would I stop when I'm on a roll?

- ❖ I just made a lot of money, so I can keep trading

- ❖ Just one or two more trades

- ❖ I know I said just one or two more, but...

Trading Addictively Without Gambling or Overtrading

If you consistently use fully developed trading systems and are therefore not gambling, you may still want to examine yourself for spiritually based addictive trading tendencies and remove any addictive spirits that you find (we will look at how to do that a bit later). Even if you are consistently profitable, you could be trading under the control of a demonically driven love of money, fear, arrogant pride, and so on.

Breaking Free From Demonic Strongholds

Okay, now let's look at a way to identify and get free from demonic strongholds. We must first understand spiritual authority and learn to hear God speak.

Three Levels of Authority

There are three major realms of authority that affect your life: first, second, and third heaven.

The first heaven is everything within earth's *physical* atmosphere. It is the earth's physical realm, as described in Genesis 2:4: *"This is the account of the heavens and the earth when they were created, in the day that the LORD God made earth and heaven."* The first heaven is the lowest level of authority. Authority and power at the highest earthly levels are still subject to the spiritual authority and power of second and third heaven.

The second heaven is everything within this world's *spiritual* atmosphere. It is this world's spiritual realm, as spoken about by Jesus in John 12:31: *"Now judgment is upon this world; now the ruler of **this world** will be cast out."* The second heaven is the middle realm of authority. Spiritual beings at the highest levels of second heaven are still subject to the authority and power of third heaven. Demonic authority can only go as high as the second heaven.

The third heaven is everything within the atmosphere of the Kingdom of God. Paul uses the term "third heaven" in Second Corinthians 12:2: *"I know a man in Christ who…was caught up to the third heaven."*

Jesus instructed us in Matthew 6:9-10 to pray that the third heaven would invade and overtake Satan's temporary occupation of earth's second heaven: *"Pray, then, in this way: 'Our Father who is in heaven, Hallowed be Your name. Your kingdom come. Your will be done, On earth as it is in heaven."* We are to facilitate the overthrow of Satan's occupying kingdom of darkness by displacing it with God's Kingdom of light.

We who are in Christ have access to operate from the third heaven. *"He [God, the Father] raised Him [Jesus] from the dead and seated Him at His right hand in the heavenly places, far above all rule and authority and power and dominion, and every name that is named, not only in this age but also in the one to come…. and raised us up with Him, **and seated us with Him** in the heavenly places in Christ Jesus"* (Ephesians 1:20-21, 2:6).

A natural person, one who has not yet been born of God's spirit, lives subject to the control of the destructive spiritual influences of Satan's earthly kingdom of darkness. Contrasting natural and spiritual people, Jesus' disciple John wrote: *"We know that we are of God, and that the whole world lies in the power of the evil one."* (1 John 5:19)

In contrast to a natural person, those who have accepted Jesus' call to a new life in a new kingdom are no longer subject to the control of this world's kingdom of darkness: *"He has delivered us from the domain of darkness and transferred us to the kingdom of his beloved Son,"* (Colossians 1:13 ESV). If you as a disciple of Jesus are unaware that God has taken you completely out from under the authority of the kingdom of darkness, you will default to believing and acting as if you are still fighting to get to a place of victory that you have already been given and from which you could be functioning.

Operations from God's kingdom override operations from first and second heaven.

Hearing God speak

Some of you may not have much experience in asking God direct questions and getting direct answers. But just as an earthly father wants to speak to his children, your heavenly Father wants to speak and communicate with you on a daily basis. Consider just the following few Scriptures about hearing God speak to us and teach us.

We hear in His Presence

*"One thing have I asked of the LORD, that will I seek after: that I may dwell in the house of the LORD all the days of my life, to gaze upon the beauty of the LORD and to **inquire** in his temple."* Psalm 27:4 (ESV)

Some versions use the word meditate instead of inquire, but the meaning remains the same: *in God's presence* we get specific answers and understanding about specific questions.

Father speaks to us

*"I will **instruct you and teach you** in the way which you should go; I will counsel you with My eye upon you."* Psalm 32:8

Holy Spirit speaks to us

*"As for you, the anointing which you received from Him abides in you, and you have no need for anyone to teach you; but as **His anointing teaches you** about all things..."* 1 John 2:27

Jesus speaks to us

*"My sheep **hear My voice**, and I know them, and they follow Me."* John 10:27

God communicates with us often and in many different ways. Just as you can develop natural skills in understanding what people are saying to you, you can develop spiritual skills in understanding what God is communicating. Maybe you have heard His voice through Scriptures or sermons, or felt Him tugging on your heart when you first gave your heart to Him, and concluded these are the only ways He will speak to you. But God can speak in many ways: through Scripture, in dreams, in visions (mental pictures like day dreams, or visions you see with your natural eyes), through your thoughts and feelings, through other people, through turning things you see into prophetic messages for you, and in many other ways. Jesus said His sheep hear His voice, so why not trust Him and be willing to hear Him in any new ways He may want to communicate with you?

As you practice the Breaking Free Steps and are asking and waiting for answers, trust that God will enable you to understand how He is speaking to you.

Breaking Free Steps

Second Corinthians 10:3-5 explains something about spiritual freedom: *"For though we walk in the flesh, we do not war according to the flesh, for the weapons of our warfare are not of the flesh, but divinely powerful for the destruction of fortresses. We are destroying speculations and every lofty thing raised up against the knowledge of God, and we are taking every thought captive to the obedience of Christ."* We are in a spiritual war—a war between Satan's occupying kingdom of darkness and God's Kingdom of light—and that war affects your trading. When a demonic spiritual stronghold is affecting your trading, you must use *spiritual* weapons to pull it down and regain your territory.

Jesus' sacrificial death on the cross defeated sin's power over you and every demonic spirit that could steal from you or bring destruction to you. But you must apply His work to the specific area in your life that needs freedom or healing; you do not automatically obtain all that belongs to you the moment you give your life to Jesus.

Here is an effective model for applying Jesus' finished work on the cross to your specific trading situations to break free from destructive spiritual strongholds within you. The Breaking Free Steps are adapted from some of the teaching and prayer models developed by Lori and Barry Byrne (*Love after Marriage workshops, http://loveaftermarriage.org/*) and Debbie and Mike Adams (*Heart of Heaven Ministries, http://www.heartofheavenministries.com/*). I have intermingled and added to their material, received as workshop handouts in 2011, with their permission. These ministries are associated with Bethel Church in Redding, California.

Prepare

Enter into God's presence. *"Where the Spirit of the Lord is, there is freedom* (2 Corinthians 3:17 ESV). This is not a formula; you are working with God. Do whatever it takes for you to connect with God at this moment. Examples:

- ❦ "Father, I come into your presence"

- ❦ Give Him thanks or praise for specific things

- ❦ Worship Him with music

- ❦ Pray with another believer or a group of believers

Identify

- ❦ Ask God, "Is there anything you want to show me that has been coming against my trading?" Wait for Him to show you.

♦ After He shows you, ask Him, "What is it trying to do, or how is it making me feel?" Wait for Him to show you.

♦ Ask God, "When did it first begin?" (If you know this, you can pull the root out.) Wait for Him to show you.

Remove

♦ "I nail _____ (what He showed you) to the cross."

♦ "I break all agreements I've made with _____, known or unknown, and I repent of joining with _____."

♦ "Father, I ask you to send _____ away from me."

Replace

Jesus explained that when demons are driven out of a place of control over a person, that place must be filled with righteousness, or the door to that newly emptied space remains open for a return of demonic influence. (See Matthew 12:43-45.)

♦ "Father, what do you give me to replace what you sent away?" Wait for Him to show you.

♦ Receive and thank Him for what He is giving you.

♦ "Father, I come into agreement with _____ and I ask that it be established as a stronghold of righteousness in me."

Record – Remove and Replace journal

You can use the following format to record the results in your *Remove and Replace* journal. As you record the results, you will be building a journal to remind yourself and reinforce what God removed, and you will also be building a toolbox of spiritual tools designed specifically for you by God. It is your responsibility to choose to use what God has given you; what He gives you may or may not automatically be established by itself.

♦ Date:

♦ What came against my trading?

♦ What did Father give me in its place?

These steps are effective, but be open to the leading of the Holy Spirit as He may direct you to do additional things.

More Specific Applications

Okay, now that you are getting familiar with some steps to obtain freedom from demonic influences, let's consider specific times and ways you could put those steps to use.

First, *when* could you use them? It would be very beneficial to go through the steps regularly at the end of every week or every trading day. You could also go through them any time during the day that you have not been trading well.

Second, you may find additional freedom by targeting each of the four chambers of your spiritual heart: your mind, will, emotions, and spirit. Spiritual strongholds or addictions can reside in any of these four areas. The mind is the thinking part of you, where truth or lies can be established. Your will is the choosing part of you, where good or bad habits can be established. Your emotions are the feeling part of you, where positive or negative associations and triggers can be established. Your spirit is the foundational core part of you, where things such as wisdom or foolishness, humility or pride, and joy or depression can reside.

To target each chamber of your heart individually, go through all the same steps, but substitute the following questions for the first question in the Identify step.

Your Mind

Ask God "Is there anything you want to show me in my *mind* that has been coming against my trading?" "What *thoughts* pull or push me into trading poorly?" You are asking God to show you things such as lies you believe about yourself, about God, about the financial markets, and other untrue things you tell yourself. What are the harmful tracks your mind automatically runs on?

Your Will

Ask God "Is there anything you want to show me in my *will* that has been coming against my trading?" "What *choices* pull or push me into trading poorly?" You are looking for things such as rebellion, disobedience, revenge, and things such as an unwillingness to take losses. What harmful choices have you predetermined to make? What beneficial choices are you unwilling to make? What are the harmful tracks your will automatically runs on?

Your Emotions

Ask God, "Is there anything you want to show me in my *emotions* that has been coming against my trading?" "What *feelings* pull or push me into trading poorly?" You are looking for negative emotions such as fear, anger, shame, or good feelings that trigger addictive trading. What are the harmful tracks your emotions automatically run on?

Your Spirit

Ask God, "Is there anything you want to show me in my *spirit* that has been coming against my trading?" "What *motivations* pull or push me into trading poorly?" You are looking for things such as the love of money, fear of displeasing people, arrogant pride, and other faulty foundations. What are the harmful tracks your spirit automatically runs on?

Establishing Righteous Strongholds

Part 1 of this book, the daily meditations and worksheets, has already addressed one way of establishing righteousness in your trading: meditating on scriptural truth and choosing to apply it to your life. And as you practice letting God identify and replace unrighteous spiritual influences with righteous spiritual influences, and continue resisting unrighteousness in your trading and agreeing with righteousness, you will be establishing strongholds of righteousness within you in an additional way.

Just as there are destructive thoughts, choices, feelings, and motivations that originate from demonic spirits, there are also *empowering* thoughts, choices, feelings, and motivations that originate from *godly* spiritual influences: either the Holy Spirit who lives inside of believers or angels sent to assist. When you come into agreement with God's empowering influences, and continue to do so, you are establishing *righteous* strongholds within you.

Scripture talks about people who are freed from sinful strongholds and then have righteous strongholds established. *"But thanks be to God that though you were slaves of sin, you became obedient from the heart to that form of teaching to which you were committed, and having been freed from sin, you became slaves of righteousness."* (Romans 6:17-18)

Slaves are compelled to do what their master wants them to do. How would you trade as a slave of righteousness? What if instead of being compelled to trade poorly, you were compelled to trade well? What if you kept adding areas in which you had an overwhelming drive to think, choose, feel, and be motivated by righteousness in your trading? Imagine being compelled to...

- ❖ Diligently complete the system development process

- ❖ Only take trades based on fully developed systems

- ❖ Risk only what is prudent per trade and per month

- ❖ Take your losses and stop trading for the day (if your loss limit is hit)

- ❖ Take your profits and stop trading for the day (if your profit limit is hit)

As you record what the Father gives you to replace destructive spiritual influences, you will build a list of specific graces God has given you to succeed in trading. You will have a tool chest full of effective spiritual tools, an arsenal filled with powerful spiritual weapons designed specifically for you by your heavenly Father. Your automatic tendencies will become increasingly righteous. Your thoughts, feelings, choices, and motivations will become aligned with God's. You will discover that God has used trading as a training ground for your whole life. You will experience *"the blessing of the LORD that makes rich, And He adds no sorrow to it."* (Proverbs 10:22) You will be a light and a blessing to your family and friends.

Staying Free

After you have invested some time identifying, removing, and replacing ungodly spiritual influences with righteous spiritual influences, you will begin to recognize destructive influences *before* you come into agreement with them. James 4:7 says, *"Submit therefore to God. Resist the devil and he will flee from you."* If you submit to God in your trading, He will be your foundation for resisting the devil in your trading. If you do not submit to God in your trading, you will be left to your own natural abilities for resisting the devil (the same condition that made you a slave of ungodly spiritual influences in the first place). You submit to God by repenting (changing your mind) from agreement with ungodly influences and by acting in agreement with God's truth and the leading of His Holy Spirit.

In addition to reinforcing righteousness in the moment of trading by acting in agreement with it, schedule a time to regularly go through the list of the trading tools (in your Remove and Replace journal) Father has been giving you. Reinforce them by reviewing them and by praying something like the following:

- ❖ "Father, I come into agreement with (something He gave you) and I ask that you would watch over me to establish it as a stronghold of righteousness in my life."

- ❖ "Since I have been set free from slavery to sin and have become a slave of righteousness, I ask that I would have an overwhelming drive to trade with (something He gave you)"

Suggested Daily Trading Routine

Here is a suggested daily routine that will help you incorporate what you have gained in this chapter into your daily trading.

1. Before trading, get into God's Presence: in worship, prayer, or meet with God somewhere in heavenly places in your imagination, by faith, or in the Spirit. For example: come boldly before the throne of grace, spoken of in Hebrews 4:16.

2. In God's presence, review with Him some entries from the journal you use to record new spiritual trading tools and come into agreement with them. "Father, I thank you for removing _____ and giving me _____ to trade with. I come into agreement with what you have given me and ask for grace to trade in fellowship with you today."

3. In fellowship with God, review rules and charts of the trade(s) you will be looking for today.

4. Trade in fellowship with God. Hunt for the best; ignore the rest.

5. After trading, record your trades in detail in fellowship with God.

6. Analyze your trades in detail in fellowship with God.

7. Go through the Breaking Free Steps, recording the results.

MAXIMIZING WISDOM

In order to have more than just a limited increase in wisdom by improving your thinking, you must receive the Spirit of Wisdom into your spirit. To be able to receive God's Spirit of Wisdom into your spirit, you must have a spiritual and personal relationship with Him. Solomon recorded that *"the LORD gives wisdom; From His mouth come knowledge and understanding"* (Proverbs 2:6). Further, Solomon declared God's wisdom superior to wisdom from any other source when he wrote, *"There is no wisdom and no understanding and no counsel against the LORD"* (Proverbs 21:30).

If you are interested in having a personal relationship with the One who gave King Solomon his wisdom, you should know that He sent His Son Jesus Christ for that very reason. Before Jesus came, God's Holy Spirit was only given to a select few. But now God's Spirit, which includes the Spirit of Wisdom, is available to all through Jesus. You can read Jesus' teachings in the Bible, in accounts written by four of his disciples: Matthew, Mark, Luke, and John.

As you read Jesus' teachings, you will see that He calls us to two foundational things that put our hearts and lives on the right course and give us the perspective to see with wisdom and understand the truth. First, He calls us to change our thinking and worldview and to choose to live in the now and eternal Kingdom of God rather than to continue living for this temporary world. Second, He calls us to choose to follow Him as a disciple by leaving our former life and way of thinking and by following Him in His way of living and thinking. You will see those two callings explained in his disciple's accounts.

You will also see that Jesus voluntarily died as a sacrifice to satisfy the eternal penalty for the sins we have all committed. We were created in God's image and designed to live connected to His love and character. But we have all acted in rebellion against God and His design for us, whether intentional or passive, with the consequences of an eternity of suffering in the darkness that exists in complete separation from God's presence and goodness. John 3:16 says, "For God so loved the world, that He gave His only begotten Son, that whoever believes in Him shall not perish, but have eternal life." His blood paid for all the wrong you have done against God, yourself, and others. The Father has provided for you to escape eternal darkness and enter into a now and eternal life in His light and presence and goodness, through accepting Jesus' sacrifice for you and answering the call to enter the kingdom of God and to be a disciple of Jesus.

As you read Jesus' teachings, the Spirit of God will begin working in your heart. Expect Jesus to meet with you and to invite you to follow Him into a new life in a new kingdom. When you have an understanding of Jesus' teachings and way of life, and would like to exchange your old way of thinking and living for His, and when you are ready to leave the dark kingdom of this world and enter God's Kingdom of light, you may want to use the following prayer as a model for declaring your intentions and as a point of accepting of His call.

Note: many who are currently Christians were taught that being born again, receiving forgiveness of sins, receiving eternal life, and receiving Jesus into their heart was essentially what it means to become a Christian. Those are all true, but they are not the two main responses Jesus expects from people who hear His teaching. Jesus primarily expects people to leave their former life and beliefs and to follow Him in His way of life and His teachings *as His disciple*, and He expects them to change their mind (repent) regarding living for this world and to choose to *live in the Kingdom of God*. If you have never fully answered these two main calls of Jesus, you can make the following prayer your own and fully establish the life Jesus called you to. You will experience greater transformation by living as a disciple of Jesus and a citizen of heaven.

"Jesus, I accept your call to follow you as a disciple and to live in the Kingdom of God. I exchange my old beliefs and way of living for your teaching and way of living. I exchange my citizenship in this world's temporary kingdom of darkness for citizenship in your eternal Kingdom of light. I believe your sacrificial death on the cross is payment in full for my sins against you, myself, and others, and I now receive the forgiveness, cleansing, healing, and freedom for which you so dearly paid. I believe that I now am born by the Spirit of God as a child of God, and you are now my Lord and my Savior. You now make me alive spiritually and fill me with your new and eternal life.

I understand that all my sins were placed on you as you voluntarily gave your life in place of mine on the cross, and that I have participated with you in death, burial, and resurrection to a new life. I am now seated with you at the Father's right hand. All I have is yours, and all you have is mine. I look forward to a life of change and growth in the days and years ahead, as you lead me in a new life with you."

Signature _____ Date _____

Jesus also was baptized and taught that we should follow him in baptism. In fact, when Jesus, and then later his disciples, preached about the kingdom of God and following Jesus, people responded not with a prayer of acceptance but by being baptized. However, a prayer will get you started in your new life until you get baptized—sort of like a driver's permit gets a new driver started before they get their permanent driver's license.

When you accept Jesus' call, a transformation will take place, a transaction in which you will join in Jesus' death on the cross and His resurrection to new life. You will be born again, made alive spiritually, as an eternal child of God. You will be forgiven for every area of your life you messed up, for every person you hurt, and for all rebellion against God, intentional or unintentional. A process of healing and growth will begin. Your old self, which was predisposed to doing wrong, will be replaced with a new self that is predisposed to doing right. You will be an entirely new creation in Jesus. God will also place His Holy Spirit in you to be your teacher and your guide, giving you motivation and ability (grace) to live righteously and fulfill your destiny.

Additionally, the blood Jesus shed in his sacrificial death for you has the power to break all that is oppressive off of you; it can set you free from the love of money, sin, addictions, rebellion, selfishness, self-hatred, unforgiveness, bitterness, and everything that destructively controls and steals life from you. When you turn your life over to God, the power of that sacrificial blood and the healing love of God are freely available to you. You might be set free and healed from some things instantly; other things may require a process or the help of other believers.

It is critical that you not try to *earn* your new life or God's love, forgiveness, or freedom; they are *gifts*. Earning them is not only impossible, but trying to earn them is an insult to all Jesus suffered as a sacrifice for your spiritual debts, to all He did to qualify you by His own work and to set you free. If we could be good enough by our natural abilities, the Father would not have had to send His Son to take away our sin and make us truly good (righteous). He loves and gives freely, so just receive.

Being born again, being made alive in your spirit, will enable you to begin living and trading from the heart. Becoming a new creation in God will create a *true* foundation for *all* aspects of your life. When you give Him the life you are powerless to keep, He will give you a life no power can take from you. He will help you guard your heart from being controlled or ruined by the love of money or by any of the many things in life He meant to be blessings. As you follow His leading, He will give you a life characterized by nobility, purpose, and fulfillment.

Just as you receive and give help by trading in community, you will receive and give help by living your new life in community (and you must find a fellowship of Christians so you can be baptized). We did not really discuss baptism, but it is *crucial* to your new life. The Christian path is almost impossible to walk without the support of like-minded people. You will find those who have also chosen to live as disciples of Jesus in Christian churches. Don't allow the bad attitudes of some individuals or churches to rob you of association with genuine followers of Jesus.

If any are curious about my personal spirituality: I am Christian, Protestant, and Charismatic. I began my relationship with God in the Church of the Nazarene, was later involved in the Vineyard Christian Fellowship, and am now a member of Bethel Church in Redding, California, a church internationally known for miraculous healings and equipping conferences.

PRAYER OF BLESSING

May you live in unbroken fellowship with God.

May you be fully trained by the spirit of the Lord, the spirit of Wisdom, the spirit of Understanding, the spirit of Counsel, the spirit of Strength, the spirit of Knowledge, and by the fear of the Lord.

May you obtain the riches, honor, and righteousness that accompanies Wisdom and may you also enjoy Wisdom's benefits that are better than gold.

May you find life and obtain favor from the Lord.

May you take part in bringing heaven to earth.

USE YOUR INFLUENCE

If you found the course helpful and think it may benefit others as well, please spread the word. Your influence can help the effort to build the number of traders who are successfully producing and using wealth to bring the blessings of God to people here on earth. Here are some suggestions:

- "Like" the *Proverbs for Traders* facebook fan page.
- Recommend the course on your favorite social networking sites.
- Write a review or testimonial on Amazon.com. These reviews are a great source of information and encouragement to potential readers. Go to the *Proverbs for Traders* page on Amazon.com and post your comments in the Customer Reviews section.
- Share your comments, experiences, suggestions for future editions, and testimonials at proverbsfortraders.com.
- Give Proverbs for Traders to a friend.
- Give Proverbs for Traders to an influential person.
- Write a review of Proverbs for Traders on a blog, magazine, or other media venue.
- Form a group of traders to go through Proverbs for Traders together.
- Register your Proverbs for Traders group and join the leaders forum at proverbsfortraders.com

START A GROUP

The benefit of reading *Proverbs for Traders* is multiplied when you turn it into a course by fully using the worksheets. Those benefits are multiplied again when you go through the course as part of a group. You cannot fully apply all sections of *Proverbs for Traders* without being part of a trading group community. Imagine the ongoing support and camaraderie you and others will have as you meet weekly, share your insights and experiences, and encourage and pray for each other. The course is quite intense, and you will be more likely to complete it and obtain wisdom and success if you go through it with others. You may even become a group of friends who choose to keep the group going after the 12 week course is over. Why not start a group?

For additional resources, free and paid, go to proverbsfortraders.com

BIBLIOGRAPHY

Adams, Mike, and Debbie Adams. "Heart of Heaven Ministries." *Heartofheavenministries*. Web. 20 Feb. 2012. <http://www.heartofheavenministries.com/>.

Byrne, Barry, and Lori Byrne. "Love After Marriage: Home." *Love After Marriage: Home*. Web. 20 Feb. 2012. <http://loveaftermarriage.org/>.

Douglas, Mark. *Trading in the Zone: Master the Market with Confidence, Discipline and a Winning Attitude*. New York: New York Institute of Finance, 2000. Print.

Edwards, Robert D., John Magee, and W. H. C. Bassetti. *Technical Analysis of Stock Trends*. 9th ed. Boca Raton, Flor.: CRC, 2007. Print.

Elder, Alexander. *Trading for a Living: Psychology, Trading Tactics, Money Management*. New York: J. Wiley, 1993. Print.

Faith, Curtis. *The Original Turtle Trading Rules*. Rep. Original Turtles. Web. 17 Oct. 2011.

Kirkpatrick, Charles D., and Julie R. Dahlquist. *Technical Analysis: the Complete Resource for Financial Market Technicians*. Upper Saddle River, NJ: FT Financial Times, 2007. Print.

Murphy, John J. *Technical Analysis of the Financial Markets: a Comprehensive Guide to Trading Methods and Applications*. New York: New York Institute of Finance, 1999. Print.

Pring, Martin J. *Technician's Guide to Day and Swing Trading*. New York: McGraw-Hill, 2003. Print.

Stoltzfus, Tony. *Leadership Coaching: The Disciplines, Skills and Heart of a Coach*. Virginia Beach, VA: T. Stoltzfus, 2005. Print.

ENDNOTES

[1] Edwards, Robert D., John Magee, and W. H. C. Bassetti, *Technical Analysis of Stock Trends*, 9th ed. Boca Raton, Flor.: CRC, 2007, Print, pages 587-588, 601

[2] Kirkpatrick, Charles D., and Julie R. Dahlquist, *Technical Analysis: the Complete Resource for Financial Market Technicians*, Upper Saddle River, NJ: FT Financial Times, 2007, Print, pages 545, 589

[3] Elder, Alexander, *Trading for a Living: Psychology, Trading Tactics, Money Management*, New York: J. Wiley, 1993, Print, page 260

[4] Murphy, John J., and John J. Murphy, *Technical Analysis of the Financial Markets: a Comprehensive Guide to Trading Methods and Applications*, New York: New York Institute of Finance, 1999, Print, pages 395-396

[5] Faith, Curtis. *The Original Turtle Trading Rules,* Rep. Original Turtles, Web. 17 Oct. 2011, page 8

[6] Kirkpatrick, page 567

[7] Murphy, page 500

Made in the USA
San Bernardino, CA
05 May 2015